Chakras for Beginners

Innovative Guide to Balance and Unblocking the Chakras and Awaken positive Energy!

Alban Kemp

Contents

Introduction

The human body has 7 main energy centers that are connected to important organs and glands of the body. It is these energy centers that are called chakras, and chakra is basically the Sanskrit word for wheel.

So the chakras in the human body are wheel-like spinning vortexes. They whirl in circular motion to create a vacuum in the center and in the process, draws everything it encounters on its independent vibratory level.

Beginners looking for more information on chakras may come across information stating that Buddhist scriptures state there are dozens of chakras while jains state there are nine chakras. They are not to be confused by this information as the most accepted chakras are the 7 chakras.

These seven charkas are not physically marked nor can they be marked or located in the human body. This is because these chakras do not belong to the physical body but are all part of the etheric or emotional body of a human being.

It can be said that it is this etheric body that is divided into various flows of energy.

1. Root chakra or Muladhara that connects us to earth. This chakra can be balanced by concentrating on basic needs like food, water, shelter and sex.

2. Sacral chakra or Swadhisthana is located below the navel and is also called hara chakra. The natural potential of it is fear, hate, anger and violence. And all this can be purified with the acceptance of one's fears.

3. Solar plexus or Manipura is the third chakra that is located at the solar plexus. This chakra exists in two forms; doubt and trust. It is when doubt is transformed that trust starts developing here.

4. Heart chakra or Anahata is the centric that divides the 7 chakras. This is the chakra that is responsible in creating balance in life. Its development leads to the feeling of more love towards others and us.

5. Throat chakra or Visshuddhi is the fifth chakra whose energy helps you grow authentic in life. Once opened, the energy in this chakra helps you communicate openly, and lets you share your perspective truthfully.

6. The third eye or Ajna is a very important chakra of the body. It is located in between the eyebrows and is considered to be the third eye of a person. It is when this third eye is opened that one starts developing awareness in themselves.

7. The crown chakra or Sahasrara is a bright white glow located at the top of your head. This is the seventh chakra that is beyond body and mind, and it is through this chakra that the body is connected to the other world.

Chakra Balancing Vs the Modern World

The modern world has brought many amazing technological advances; but at the same time, it has led to a loss of awareness on the part of many people of the importance, even the existence of their spiritual welfare.

We can learn a lot from Hindu philosophy, which has kept this knowledge of the vital role played by our spiritual beings to our overall health alive in a changing world.

Our body contains 7 vital energy centers and many secondary ones. These energy centers are known as Chakras and their proper function is essential to our physical, mental and spiritual health.

When our Chakras are out of balance, it has a negative impact on our health. This makes Chakra balancing a vital element of maintaining proper health.

You can think of your Chakras as the gates which regulate the flow of energy in and out of the body. These centers are located along the spine - from the base to the top of your head, the seven primary Chakras take in and emit energy form the world around us.

✓ What causes distortion in the Chakras?

When your Chakras are blocked, the flow of this energy is disturbed and this can have a serious effect on your health; even physical health.

Chakric function can be disturbed by poor physical health and diet, stress, bottled up emotions and a number of other factors; thankfully, all of these can be corrected.

✓ Chakra Balancing is the Key to Better Health and Greater Happiness

People who have been aware of the Chakras have always sought to keep them properly balanced in order to achieve peak physical, mental and spiritual health. Self-healing is something you may have heard about before - this is a methodology based on the idea of Chakra balancing.

Our Chakras are responsible for many aspects of our health - the workings of our endocrine system, the diseases which may affect is and our thought processes. Chakra balancing can make sure that all of the systems of our physical body are working properly and that our mental health is in proper balance.

How the Spine and the Chakras Connect

The spine is part of the physical body and the chakras are part of the energetic body but these bodies are not separate from each other. They connect like a hologram, overlapping and intertwining together as the chakras align along the length of the spine. There are minor chakras or energy centres that link with the vertebrae which make up the boney structure of the spine. They also link with the tendons, ligaments and muscles that support and move the spine. Each vertebrae and surrounding connective tissue has its very own corresponding energy centre.

Each section of the spine also corresponds with the seven major chakras.

The major chakras that align with the Cervical Spine (neck) are the throat, brow and crown chakras. Through the Thoracic Spine (mid & upper back) are the heart and solar plexus chakras. Finally at the

Lumbar Spine (lower back) are the sacral and base chakras.

As well as being connected physically and symbolically with the body, the chakras relate to particular life lessons or issues that we may be exploring.

Base of the spine: Base Chakra - Stability and safety; feet on the ground; trust versus fear; the physical body; the material world.

Lower back: Sacral Chakra - Relationships; finance; sexuality; creativity; the birth of new ideas.

Middle back: Solar Plexus - Seat of personal power; control; "Make it real".

Upper back between the shoulder blades: Heart - Seat of all emotion; your Truth.

Neck (cervical spine) : Throat Chakra - Your will; communication of your Truth.

Base of the skull: Brow Chakra - Intuition; assimilation; perspective.

Top of the skull: Crown Chakra - Sense of purpose; connection with Source; ability to see the bigger picture.

The connection between the two is not just isolated to their physical placement in relation to each other, it is very much a connection that is reliant on and reflected by each other. Any holding or tension at the physical level will slow the free flow of energy through the chakras and any discourse through the chakras will impact on the movement and mobility of the spine.

Therefore to achieve a sense of balance through both we must recognise they are intrinsically connected and sustained through movement and at its most effective, movement that is without impingement, restriction or limitation.

When we physically move to flexion at the spine and bend forwards we close the front of the body and open the back of the body but we also contract the front of our energy centres and expand through the back. Symbolically, this movement connects us with what is in the past or what is behind us. Through flexion we not only allow ourselves a means of stretching and opening to our past experiences, we also experience what it is to collapse, close down and fold in upon our energetic selves with inner enquiry.

As we physically return to upright, in extension, we explore what it means to support our structure with stability and balance. Our energy centres, front and back also respond to the sense of this return to balance.

When we hyper-extend(bend backwards) we are opening the front of the body and closing the back of the body. By opening through the front of our chakras we are expanding energetically, outward looking and forward looking. Symbolically we are welcoming whatever the future may bring.

Through a side bend (lateral flexion) we are physically able to experience a more creative way of moving that is not typically found on a daily basis. Our sides are usually working hard, fixed, stabilising and holding. As the spine, tendons and ligaments are encouraged to release in a creative way to the side, so is our corresponding chakra energy.

All of these physical movements give us a means to connect and work with bringing our energy and chakras, via the body, in to free flow and balance.

To ensure this release and free flow of energy is continual and nurturing we could be exploring the full range of movement that is available to us through the spine on a daily basis.

A further fundamental connection between maintaining the spine and the chakras is the movement of rotation.

Physically, we are capable of rotation or twisting to varying degrees through the different sections of the spine. This twisting is mirrored in the movement of our chakra (or kundalini) energy twisting up in a spiral from the base of the spine to the top of the head.

Through the Lumbar spine where the vertebrae are bigger and their primary function is to stabilise there is 5 degrees of rotation available to us. Any loss in this degree of rotation will impact on our ability to trust, feel grounded and safe. Subsequently lower back muscles tense up to reinforce the support for the body so we feel safe again. If we are encountering difficulties in our relationships this too will impact on this area of the back. Over time these muscles become tighter and more tense. The loss of physical movement continues and the movement of energy becomes slower, even stagnant through the sacral chakra and the base chakra.

It seems important to acknowledge that because there is little rotation available here, any loss will have significant impact on us.

Through the Thoracic spine where the vertebrae are functioning somewhat to stabilise but also to provide more mobility there is 35 degrees of rotation available to us. Here the chakras speak of our heart's story and how we enforce it with our solar plexus and our personal power. Represented by either collapsing postures as we shut down our heart or with our chest thrust forwards to do battle with the world. Rotation and thus liberation quickly becomes lost and inaccessible within these patterns of holding. It may even cause us deeper pain, physically, to try to free ourselves energetically, through movement.

Finally, through the Cervical spine where the vertebrae provide us with the most mobility there is 50 degrees of rotation available to us. This enables us to have good all round vision from one shoulder all the way through the front to arrive at the other shoulder and, via the crown chakra, the ability to see the bigger picture and have a sense of something greater. The throat chakra is also connected to the cervical spine. This chakra is most strongly linked with communicating your Truth. Any difficulty in speaking your Truth will result in tension and holding through the throat and neck and even the jaw. Over time this will cause restriction in the range of movement and even loss of movement through the cervical spine as that sense of freedom and mobility to speak your Truth becomes more and more stifled. A fixed cervical spine will lead to a narrowing of your field of vision as you no longer have the ability to move your head from side to side. The impact of this on your brow chakra (also linked with the cervical spine) is hugely symbolic as your actual field of vision narrows leaving you literally with a narrowing perspective on the world. The loss of cervical rotation then slows down the energy of the crown through which we have our connection with source. We struggle to see the bigger picture and have a sense of something greater.

To sustain and nurture the free flowing connection between our spinal health and our energetic health we would benefit greatly from some form of movement that is outside of our daily norm.

Using Healing Crystals - A Guide to Chakras and Gemstones

Healing crystals are those that bring therapeutic value to the areas of your life that bring you discomfort or suffering. These could be minor physical ailments, such as headaches, through to emotional matters such as stress. Healing crystals can help you to unblock your negative energies and allow positive ones to flow through you again. Here are some examples of how to work with crystals and some of the best ones to use.

Chakra can be translated from the Sanskrit word for wheel, which illustrates the movements around these points. Energy doesn't like to stay still! There are 7 chakra points, starting with the root chakra at the base of the spine and going up to above the top of your head. The energies within these chakras vibrates at various speeds and it is important to ensure that this does not become blocked. If this happens, the individual will feel an imbalance and possibly a range of symptoms to go with it.

Healing crystals can help to unblock the chakras and restore you to a feeling of balance and calm. A full list of which crystals can be used for each chakra is beyond the scope of this article, but here are some suggestions:

1st Chakra - smokey quartz

2nd Chakra - tiger's eye

3rd Chakra - citrine

4th Chakra - rose quartz

5th Chakra - sodalite

6th Chakra - clear quartz

7th Chakra - amethyst

✓ Top 5 Favourite Healing Crystals

There are other ways to use healing crystals however. Here are my favourite 5 and some suggestions of what you might use them for:

✓ Amethyst

This gemstone is a wonderful talisman and so to gain its protection for the whole day, it is very effective worn as jewellery.

✓ Citrine

It is a very tough stone but a lively one, raising your spirits when you're feeling low and giving you pep when feeling listless.

✓ Tiger's Eye

Traditionally used to ward off curses. However it can also be used to help you to recognise your own potential.

✓ Rose Quartz

Such a pretty stone, how can it be for anything but love!

✓ Hematite

To encourage the flow of energy through the chakras, it unblocks you and helps you to regain your strength after a difficult time.

Understanding Chakras and Methods of Chakra Balancing

The purpose of chakra balancing, otherwise known as chakra awakening, is to balance energy in the body. Your energies exist and function much like your physical body does. When one aspect is damaged or blocked, it can affect your emotional health as well. Chakras are focal points for your energies, starting at your head and descending down your spine.

There are seven generally recognized chakras.

First: The root chakra is located at the base of your spine and is red in color. It deals with survival issues, such as food, money and basic comfort. Keeping the root chakra balanced is a key component in maintaining a balanced life. When fundamental aspects of your life seem out of joint, focusing on your root chakra is the first place to start healing.

Second: The sacral chakra is located in the lower abdomen and is orange in color. Its element is water, and it focuses on sexual relationships, pleasure, friendship and personal wellbeing.

Third: The solar plexus chakra is in the upper abdomen and is yellow in color. Its element is fire and it links to the energetic state of the physical and emotional body. A healthy solar plexus chakra provides you with the willpower, focus and confidence to pursue your goals.

Fourth: The heart chakra is right in the middle of your chest. Its color is green and its element is air. Many consider it the most important of the focal points, as it focuses on your connection with all of humanity. As your heart chakra opens, you are able to freely express feelings of gratitude and love.

Fifth: The throat chakra (located in your throat) is bright blue in color. It rules speech, sound and communication. An open throat chakra enables you to express your feelings and thoughts in a healthy way.

Sixth: One of the most well-known chakras, the third eye is on your forehead between your eyes. Its color is indigo blue, and it relates to your intuition and your ability to see beyond the physical. This chakra directly affects your imagination, wisdom and decision-making abilities.

Seventh: The crown chakra is located on top of your head. Its color is purple, and it is the creative center where you connect with your higher self. A balanced crown chakra enhances your appreciation of the divine intelligence in the universe.

Your chakras are intertwined, so when one of them is blocked, the cascading effects can be extremely detrimental. Think of your physical body like the hardware of a computer; it's a functional machine that runs as long as it is maintained and has power (such as food, drink, etc.). A computer cannot function without the proper software. Your chakras function like the computer's software, harnessing its power for specific purposes. Just like a computer, your energy system can pick up damaging energies. Chakra balancing works similarly to a virus detection program, cleansing the system to avoid long-term damage.

✓ There are several recommended techniques of chakra balancing.

Hands-on: A hands on approach is a traditional approach to balancing chakras. It requires a detailed understanding of how the chakras relate to one another, so it's often recommended that you go to a professional.

Emotional Freedom Technique: Emotional Freedom Technique (EFT) involves tapping key energy points on your body and reciting affirmations and resolutions.

Gemstones: Gemstones are often used to cleanse and activate chakras. You place specific stones on each one of them and chant special mantras, known as seed sounds,

Meditation: Meditation is the simplest and one of the most effective methods. It involves being in a relaxed physical state while focusing on a specific chakra.

Balanced chakras can enable you to connect more easily with goals that feel right for you on a deeply emotional level.

Chakra Stones: Chakra stones are a specific system of chakra balancing. You place a specific stone (each chakra has one) on one chakra, and you meditate.

Meditation: Meditation is the simplest and one of the most effective methods of chakra balancing. It involves a relaxed physical state, coupled with focused attention on a specific chakra.

Chakra Balance and Automatic Chakra Balance

Chakras are not some mysterious elements of Eastern culture. Chakras are not just for spiritual gurus or those wanting to raise their kundalini energy. We all need to be aware of chakras and how to balance them. Among other things, these are our "filters." When our chakras are out of balance, our lives become out of balance. Does your car operate better with its tires aligned and balanced or not? Chakras are part of our body, just as teeth are part of our body. We need to learn how to care for our chakras just as we would any other part of our body. Doing so brings balance to our lives.

We have our physical bodies that we can see, feel, touch, and we have our spiritual bodies, which surround our physical bodies. The chakras are contained in our spiritual bodies/energy field/aura, which we are not so acutely aware of because we cannot so readily see, feel, and touch these in the same way. But they are definitely there and are designed to work in concert with our physical bodies, just as a knee is designed to work with a leg, and an arm with a shoulder. As so, they are indeed an important part of our bodies.

Each chakra contains or houses certain energy and each is a different color. For example, in the root chakra is contained the energy of money, the energy of family, of tribe, of self-worth, of abuse, and self-abuse, of addiction, of money as it relates to self-worth. The seeds of the energy of creation live here as well. Any energy that is "base" or "root" resides in the first chakra. The color of the root chakra is red.

One of the reasons that it's important to know this information and know how to balance your chakras is for purposes of manifesting and trying to use the Law of Attraction. If we know now that the energy of money is in the root chakra, how do you suppose you're going to manifest anything with just the power of your mind? The power of the mind is the 6th chakra. The energy of what you're trying to manifest doesn't live in the mind. It lives in the root.

To manifest and co-create you're going to have to figure out how to connect the energy that resides in all of the chakras, not just, for example, put all your "thinking" energy on money and expect it to poof into your world. This is one very good reason to want to balance your chakras. By doing so, you can learn to harness all of the power that resides in all of the chakras and begin to connect the energy of all of those. "You can begin to connect the dots." And then watch your life change for the better. Balancing your chakras brings you back into a place of reclaiming your personal power and helps you align with your life's purpose.

Chakra balance is often perceived as "work," just as things like meditation are also perceived as "work." I've developed a special method for chakra balance, Automatic Chakra BalanceTM, that uses certain elements such as music, sound, and visuals to help you balance your energy field. Every musical note corresponds to and resonates with a different chakra and different visuals stimulate certain parts of the psyche. Combining these in specific ways and in certain patterns, results in "automatic" energy field shift.

Nutrition and the Chakra System

Protein supports the base chakra by providing the solid tissue of the body, maintaining it through repairs and digestion and protecting it through immunity. Protein is made of a chain of amino acids. The amino acids are connected by a peptide bond into dipeptide (two amino acids), tripeptide (three amino acids) and ploypeptide (more than three amino acids) chains. The amino acids are unstable compounds. They need to attach to others chemicals to be complete, so the amino acids in a chain are unique. It is the unique combination of amino acids and the way that the chain is shaped that determine its function and its characteristics.

Protein in our bodies is built from the protein we eat. The protein we ingest loses its shape and identity through being digested. The polypeptide chains are pulled apart by stomach acid and enzymes in the small intestine back into amino acids. These amino acids are absorbed through the small intestine and sent to various parts of the body to be used in protein synthesis. Good sources of protein include all animal products, legumes, grains and many vegetables. Meat provides the highest quantity and quality of protein, but eating a combination of other high protein foods will also supply the body with a balanced array of amino acids. For example rice and beans, a traditional food in India, China and South America provide a complete group of amino acids. Eating enough protein helps to support the function of the base chakra.

Just as Muladhara begins our physical manifestation in the womb, DNA prescribes all of the characteristics that are being formed by informing the ribosome (protein manufacturers of the cell) of how to put together and shape the protein. These characteristics will define the protein and its purpose. Protein collagen lays the groundwork for the bones as they develop and grow, it is the intercellular glue of the artery walls; and scars, tendons and ligaments are all made of collagen. Protein keratin fills our skin cells creating a solid barrier against our body and everything else. Protein is a structural component of all our organs and our muscles.

Balance Your Chakras With Acupuncture and Essential Oils

Chakra acupuncture combines the wisdom of ancient Indian medical knowledge and Chinese acupuncture. In Indian traditional medicine (such as Ayurvedic medicine), the chakras are seven key energy centers. The word comes from the Sanskrit for 'wheel of light'. In contemporary alternative therapies the two systems have been usefully combined, both in reaching a diagnosis and in treatment. Aromatherapy and the use of essential oils add a third level to this way of healing.

The seven principal chakras, or energy centers, are the material incarnation of the spiritual. They are located on the midline of the body, in line with the spine from the cranium to the groin area. There are many more chakras, but these seven - the root, spleen, solar plexus, heart, throat, third eye, and crown chakras - are the most important. The chakras correspond more or less to the 'organs' in Chinese medical terminology. The fourth chakra, for example, correlates with the liver and spleen in Chinese medicine. The different chakras are foci for different types of power and consciousness, such as personal power (third chakra), sexual potency (second chakra) and creative energy (fifth chakra).

The chakras are not only concerned with the flow of energy in the body but also with mediating positive and negative energy from the surrounding environment, that affects physical, emotional and spiritual health. Chakra imbalances are caused by stress, illness, poor nutrition and social and spiritual problems, amongst other things. Similarly to traditional Chinese medicine, acupuncture is concerned both with energy locations and the flow of energy, or qi, along channels or meridians. Yin and yang are the positive and negative forces of qi. Both acupuncture and the chakra circulatory system aim to restore balance, to release energy blockages .

Chakra acupuncture brings together the power of the two systems. Acupuncture needles inserted at the chakra locations are believed to achieve the aim of revitalizing the life forces and unblocking the energy channels.

The philosophy of aromatherapy, using essential oils, complements Ayurvedic and Chinese medicine still further. The oil can be inhaled, applied to the hands or feet, matched to the particular chakra that needs re-balancing or simply placed within the patient's energy field. The specific oil used may also be chosen according to principles of color therapy, with different colors corresponding to different chakras and their particular energies. Different oils also have differing energizing effects.

The three therapies combine seamlessly and for many offer the answer to their physical and emotional needs. Like other alternative ways of healing, chakra acupuncture with aromatherapy is a drug-free health path that takes into account that we are not just biological organisms but also spiritual beings.

Use Of Chios Field For Energy Healing

Energy healing -aura and chakra healing- is one of the most profound and beneficial therapies in the field of medicine and holistic health. It is about spiritual, mental, physical and emotional healing. Energy healing is a wide term. It includes various modules from holistic healing to crystal healing, Reiki to Ki and Chios healing. Energy healing uses the aura of body and environment to heal a person. It is the most natural form of therapy. It creates awareness in the healer and the patient. It answers the questions that human could not find answer to.

Chios energy field healing is a new development in energy healing. Chios healing deals with healing aura and chakra to provide relief from pain. The practitioners finds out about the imbalance in the field of aura, such as impurities, blockages, leak, fears, under-charged chakra. The Chios energy healer with steady practise and balanced chakras learns to find out the imbalance in anyone else's chakra or aura and then the root cause of the problem to apply the Chios energy healing technique.

Energy healing in general is based on the idea that physical and emotional ailments have a spiritual element that can be healed, helping to bring healing to the related physical and emotional elements as well. All that we experience is positive ions flowing in our energetic field. When this field becomes blocked, or damaged by strong negative emotions, such as anger, fear, frustration or anxiety, physical symptoms start manifesting in various forms like depression, fever, body aches. Healing at the level of aura and chakras will help to prevent future ailments and make you healthy and fit in mental as well as physical terms.

Chios energy healing uses light, colors and visualization effects to heal energy field. Chios healing requires three attunement, once you are finished with level 1, then you move to the second level.

Chios practitioners channel the energy and directs it towards the person in need to heal from the defect. Chios healing has only one version of healing. Person practicing Chios develops the ability to see the auric fields and energy and have higher intuitive abilities as a result of learning Chios.

To treat blocked chakras using the light, perform the unblocking technique as usual, but also visualize the cloud of light below your palms and at the same time visualize the appropriate symbol composed of the light. See the light also, as the energy flow into and upwards through the chakra, as it becomes unblocked. See the light as the energy that would flow through a clear chakra, and visualize the chakra clearing in this way.

To seal leaks or tears using the light, for example, perform the technique as usual, but also visualize a brilliant layer of light just below your open palm, fusing shut and sealing the break as you move the hand over the damaged area of the field-like a surgeon using a laser.

The Chakra Clearing Meditations

Whenever we are facing many stresses in life, or are not taking good care of ourselves, our chakras (the energy centers of our body) become blocked or clouded. We begin to feel worn down, stressed out, and sometimes become more negative than we need to or should be. Thus, it might be time to get ourselves involve with a little chakra clearing meditation.

The art of chakra clearing meditation helps you to become centered, balance, and clear by focusing on each of the eight chakras that are found within the body. It is a technique that is natural and practiced an as alternative healing therapy. The main purpose of it is to gain a healthy sense of well-being through clearing your mind and self-analysis with simple meditation techniques.

✓ So how does one go about doing this technique?

First, you need to get your body into a relaxed state. Then you need to mentally focus on each of your major chakras located in your body. In order to do this, you will have to use your intuition to see if you can see the colors of the chakras, and feel if there are any energy blockages. If you find a blockage, mentally unblock and erase it from your mind by breathing out slowly and imagining how the negative energy escapes your body. It could include grinding them out into the ground when you breathe out.

The key to remember about chakras is that when in harmony and in balance they help the body function well. When out of balance, even if it is just one chakra, it will affect the others. Depending on how bad the blockage or how sick or unstable we are, it can affect us pretty severely if we are not careful. That is why chakra meditation is so important. Once you are comfortable enough slowly open your eyes and be in stillness. When you are ready, stand up, stretch, and move around.

When first practicing and learning about this meditation, it is vital to learn about what your chakras are and how they function so that you can learn about how your energy reacts within and those around you. You can also learn about chakra clearing meditation from many resources that explain in detail how the technique works. You will learn the proper way to practice as well as the proper techniques. When you do this, you will breathe out negative energy and breathe in the positive.

The Chakras and Energy Streams

Every chakra in the body has a particular vibration connected to one of the colors of the spectrum. The chakra takes in the color energy from the aura that envelopes the body. The other colors are assigned to their respective energy centers, which are located within the spine.

Seven chakras make up the body, serving as the essential managers of energies that go in and out of the body. Even if the chakras are not physically visible in the body, they are related to the fields of energy that surround the body. To aid in making the energy of the chakras balanced, the Chakra Jewelry and Chakra Light Catchers has been created.

Chakras energize the physical body and are related to the interactions of the mind and body. These energy centers are regarded as loci of prana or life energy that flow along the nadis or pathways.

A stream of energy enters the body in the chakras. The same energy stream seeps into the universe, the deities, and the "subtle bodies." The nadis, which are represented as veins, nerves, and tubes in the Indian tradition, connects the different chakras. There are an infinite number of chakras. The channels are related to divine harmonies so that the following can be created: colors, geometry, elements, and streams of energy, among others.

When two persons engage in sex, the lights from their sex chakras are combined. Then the purple light waves make figures, whose beauty depends on the kind and intensity of love between the two partners. If two people really love each other, they make a great aura around them while they are having sex. The aura is comparable to the purple forest of fairytale trees with leaves and flowers that form an arc above the two partners. This creates powerful vibrations that burn away negative karmas. Simply loving a person and showing this love through sex that is satisfying can develop anyone personally and spiritually.

Chakras and Health: What You Should Know

Chakra work consists of numerous methods, but all have the same goal: the transformation of the energy functions of the chakras and the harmonization of the flow of energy between them. This is of the utmost importance. When the circulation of energy is unbalanced or obstructed, countless problems can develop; including psychological problems.

The origin of many of our problems dwells in the energy centers and the circulation of energy through the body.

✓ Health and Well Being Through Chakra Therapy

The state of the chakras affects all of our organs, the skeleton, and the hormonal, digestive, circulatory and nervous systems- in short, the entire organism. Chakra teaching asseverates that behind every ailment lies a problem with the level or flow of energy and that this leads to a perturbation in the body's natural balance.

✓ Total Healing

Holistic healing approaches such as chakra-oriented therapy are not directed toward alleviating illness-although that may be the initial reason we turn to them. For true healing to take place, the deeper reasons for sickness must be addressed. The healing process implicates not only the alleviation of symptoms but an inner freeing, a maturation, that restores a healthy equilibrium. As we know from the study of psychosomatic conditions, such complaint as stomach troubles, asthma, and high blood pressure are often connected to emotional struggles.

Everybody go through this at one time or another. We are more susceptible to colds when we are stressed, and anyone who is prone to allergies knows that they become aggravated when we are tense and cranky. Chakra teaching takes this a step further and points out that many other sicknesses have their roots in deeper levels of our being. Emotional illnesses have causes that are related to a lack of serenity, inner strength and peace. When our spiritual goal is obstructed and the energy transmitted by the chakras does not flow freely, it burdens our spirits, our minds and lastly our bodies.

Stomach disorders, for example, often develop from spiritual and mental troubles that stem from trying to stamp down irritation and a tendency to anger. The basic problem is that energy is not circulating as it should be, and as a result the relationship with our higher self is lost. Chakra therapy aims at healing these energetic disorders. It works to bring order to the assorted levels of energy. At the same time, it can amplify our awareness and lead us to deeper levels of consolidation and understanding.

To succeed at the true causes of our physical ailments, it is helpful to reckon the different areas of the body that are governed by each of the chakras. By considering why you experience from a particular illness, you can gain valuable insights. The concern with deeper causes of ill health always leads to increased self-awareness.

Fascinating facts about health affecting each chakra:

✓ A person with a healthy root chakra stands with both feet firmly on the ground.

✓ A strong sacral chakra helps in detoxifying the body, fortifies the immune system, and results in the health of the reproductive system and sexual organs.

✓ The digestive system and the control of body temperature are subject upon the navel chakra.

✓ Someone with a well-developed heart chakra usually has a salubrious heart, strong lungs, and good blood circulation.

✓ A strong voice and healthy breathing are signs of a well-developed throat chakra.

✓ People with strong forehead chakras often don't need eyeglasses and/or hearing aids, even when they grow old.

✓ A strong crown chakra is an assurance of good health. But if blocked it can result in serious illness.

Chakra and the Energy Within Yourself!

Chakra is a traditional concept that originally appeared in the Sanskrits (Indian sacred writing). Today it is used to explain a belief in health and wellness that science fails to completely describe.

There are a lot of writings about chakra and the concept actually transgresses throughout religion, energy and health. We will concentrate more on its relation to the human body.

Chakra is energy that links human's body, mind and soul into one. Writings about this mystical belief prove that chakra is a center of convergence for life energy for all humans. There are six (or seven in other writings and beliefs) chakra points in the human body, and each point corresponds to a point where we assimilate, receive and manifest energy.

Chakra centers are located on different centers of the spine. It branches throughout our body starting at the bottom of the spinal column and up towards the top of our skull.

The primary chakra is called the muladhara chakra. It is in the lower part of your body. Spiritual belief expresses that every human being has knowledge and control of this energy point.

Next chakra point is the swadhisthana. It is located in the reproductive organs of humans. Knowledge or control of this chakra enables you to attain sexual control and supreme satisfaction in sex.

The manipura chakra is also known as the navel chakra. It, as the name suggests is in the navel or abdomen part of the human body. It corresponds to knowledge and control of hunger and other human feelings associated with this body part.

The heart chakra or anahata chakra is the center that is often unopened or untouched by a lot of people. It corresponds to general emotions like pain, love, anger and others. Controlling this chakra point means that you control your emotion, and despite outside factors, your emotions remain stable.

The vishuddha chakra or the throat chakra corresponds to speech. Knowledge, diction and wisdom through words result if one has control of this energy point. Public speakers, politicians and debaters are believed to have mastered this chakra, both knowingly and unknowingly.

The anja or eyebrow chakra corresponds to higher energy level. Mastering this chakra means that you as a person will be able to see things differently. Visionaries, as well people with low psychic power and intelligence are believed to have unlocked the mysteries of this chakra.

The last and inarguably the highest level of chakra is the one located in the top of your head. The sahasrara chakra corresponds to supreme intelligence. Chakra believes insist the unlocking this chakra is almost impossible to a lot of people. Only the true geniuses and those with unselfish dedication to the Hindu discipline can unlock it. Others however believe that opening this chakra points means you have transgressed the boundaries of the human mind. Many still believe that this is the third eye chakra, giving you supreme perception ability and even clairvoyance. Possessing the key to this chakra point means that you can understand and interpret more than your eyes can see.

Chakra Balancing - The Seven Chakras and Why It's So Very Important For Good Health

Many people do not understand the role of the chakras, how or why they are needed. The seven Chakras are the main energy centers of the body. A complete Chakra Balancing session involves the seven major chakras, which balances and cleanses each chakras, so the natural energy flows freely through the body without disturbances or blockages. These blockages can e lead to physical, mental, emotional and spiritual unease.

The body contains a number of energy centers called chakras which control the distribution of energy throughout the whole body. There are seven chakras which are the major chakra and also many smaller chakras, operating within the human body and extend out into the aura.

The chakra centers heal the body and often become unbalanced in many people on a regular basis. Following a chakra healing, it is possible to bring the seven chakras back into correct alignment.

Chakra healing can be achieved by a using number of different healing modalities such as:

1. Meditation
2. Visualization
3. Reiki
4. Crystals
5. Yoga
6. Tai chi,
7. Color therapy
8. Yoga
9. Aromatherapy

Although most people cannot see the chakras with the human eye, they do control the primary function of the body. Clairvoyants, Psychics, and healing therapists can visibly see the chakras and see and feel the color and the rate that they are spinning. It is not necessary to be able to see the chakras to perform a chakra healing on yourself.

When the chakras are perfectly aligned, clear and unblocked it enables one to feel well and enjoy optimal health. The chakras are connected to both the physical body and organs and also the different layers in our subtle bodies or sometimes called the Aura. Each Chakra has its own color and is related to different layers of the outer physical body.

Color Guide Chakra of the Seven Major Chakras :

The Root Chakra: This is the physical layer - Red

The Spleen Chakra: This is the emotional layer - Orange

The Solar Plexus Chakra: This is the mental or intellectual layer - Yellow

The Heart Chakra: This is the astral layer. - Green

The Throat Chakra: This is the etheric layer - Blue

The Brow Chakra: The "Third Eye" is the celestial layer. Indigo

The Crown Chakra: This is the ketheric layer - Violet

The seven chakras are an amazing yet vital part of the human body. They spin clockwise and anticlockwise and they can also be open or closed. Not all chakras spin at the same rate either. Unbalanced or dirty chakras can result in stress, emotional turmoil, anxiety, pain, discomfort, illness and disease. Blocked chakras cause the organs and glands to act sluggish or malfunction.

Chakra Balancing - Easy Ways To Bring Balance To Your Chakras

Chakra balancing takes constant work, as there are numerous ways that can draw them out of balance if you do not pay enough attention. There are many ways to help your chakras achieve balance such as Reiki healing chakras, color therapy, aromatherapy and balancing with the help of crystals or gemstones.

Meditation is the number one technique in helping the whole energy gets back into balance. You will observe changes in how you feel if you will take time to meditate daily. It will become easier as you get better in healing chakra meditation. You will realize that you are beginning to understand more about yourself and your spirituality.

If your chakras need some improving, taking a shower flushes your energetic system. This may sound a little simple but it can be very effective and powerful. Water is so very vital to our bodies. Another really good tip is drinking water. Having a physically healthy body is really important. It keeps your healing chakras and healing auras healthy too. Energy will then run appropriately throughout your whole system

Get in the lifestyle of being active. In chakra balancing, you will get a better chance to keep your chakras, cleansed, clear and balanced which will assist in maintaining your body physically, mentally and emotional balanced and consequently you will feel healthy and happy.

Color therapy also helps in chakra balancing. If you have a certain chakra that requires balancing or healing, include the colors into your life. Wear the color; eat foods that are the color, get healing stone chakras that are related to it.

Chakra bracelets, necklaces and pendants are also a good in keeping your chakras balanced the whole day. Although when you wear chakra bracelets and crystals do remember to cleans them regularly as they too can easily absorb negative energy.

Crystal Healing can be also used for balancing the seven chakras. The purpose of using healing crystals chakras is to revive the balance of elusive energies and to return the physical being to a healthy state. Crystal is a solution to alternative medicine, an ideal way for alternative treatments.

Natural medicine chakras acknowledge that a chakra which is not balanced, can allow disharmony in the physical body which can cause illness.

All these different ways combined together helps in the treatment of various conditions, and the achievement of emotional health through chakra balancing of the seven chakras.

Crystals for Chakra Balancing

Just like you carry a few everyday items in your purse, pocket or car, like cough drops to soothe your throat, lip gloss to protect and brighten your lips or gym shoes for your lunchtime walk, having a set of crystals can be very useful for clearing energy blockages and opening chakras.

They need not be fancy or showy and seem to work best when they are allowed to choose you. As proof that "everything" in this life is alive, aware and responsive, hold your hand over a few crystals and wait until one or more of them signals you that they are ready to become yours, to accompany you and to work with you by both absorbing and giving off energy.

Now, as the new guardian of your crystals and the recipient of their marvelous power, you have a responsibility to keep them clean and energized. First steep your new crystals overnight in a solution of sea salt and water and dry them thoroughly before you begin to use them.

Periodically, re-wash your crystals in the salt solution, or in rainwater and then re-energize them by exposing them to moon or sunlight for several hours. Take advantage of the healing energy of every full moon by leaving your crystals outside overnight.

Crystals can be simple, yet powerful tools when you're seeking balance and a sense of well-being in your physical, mental, emotional and spiritual self.

To aid in general stress relief, try placing three clear quartz crystals, points facing outward, in a triangle just below your navel. Next, place three rose quartz stones in an arc above your pubic bone and relax for 4-5 minutes. Repeat as often as is needed for optimal energy flow.

For a complete Chakra Balance, try this simple crystal layout to reinforce your chakra energies and ensure they are functioning well.

Choose a grounding stone (black, brown or dark red) to place between your feet.

Then choose a stone or crystal corresponding to the different colors of the chakras, placing the red one between your knees, the orange right above your pelvic bone, the yellow right above your navel, the green over your heart center, the light blue on your throat, indigo or dark blue on your forehead and a violet or clear stone on the floor just above the top of your head. Lie down with these stones in place for a period of about 5 minutes or until you feel complete, then remove the stones starting with the one above your head.

Chakras - How Do They Affect Our Psychic Mind?

Chakras are energy wheels/centers within the body. When chakras are clean and healthy, energy flows freely within the body. When our chakras are unbalanced, we experience disease in the body. As all mind/body/spirit systems are connected and interrelated, dis-ease in one area will encourage dis-ease in the others.

When we keep our chakras balanced and cleansed, we support our physical, mental, emotional and spiritual health. Clear and balanced chakras support a clear and balanced psychic mind. Cleansing and balancing the chakras can be done through prayer, intention, visualization and by calling on non-physical beings such as Archangels Metatron and Michael as well as Melchizedek (a Judaic and New Age master).

Each chakra correlates to major nerve ganglia branching forth from the spinal column. In addition, chakras also correlate to levels of consciousness, archetypal elements, the developmental stages of life, colors, sounds and body functions. Here are the chakras:

✓ Base Chakra = Earth, Physical Identity, Self-preservation-Red

Located at the base of the spine, this chakra forms our foundation. It is related to our survival instincts (food, shelter, money, etc.), our sense of grounding and our connection to our physical bodies. When healthy this chakra attracts health, prosperity and security.

✓ Sacral Chakra = Water, Emotional Identity, Self-gratification-Orange

Located a few inches above the base chakra (lower back, sexual organs) this chakra relates to emotions and sexuality. It connects us to others through feelings, desires, sensations and movement. When healthy, this chakra brings us fluidity, grace, sexual fulfillment and the ability to accept change.

✓ Solar Plexus Chakra = Fire, Ego Identity, Self-definition-Yellow

Located in the solar plexus area, this chakra relates to personal power, will, autonomy and metabolism. When healthy, this chakra brings us energy, effectiveness, spontaneity and non-dominating power.

✓ Heart Chakra = Air, Social Identity, Self-acceptance, Love-Green

Located near the heart, this chakra is in the middle of the seven chakras and is related to love. It is also the integrator of mind & body, male & female, persona & shadow, ego & unity. When healthy, this chakra allows us to love deeply, feel compassion and have a deep sense of peace and centeredness.

✓ Throat Chakra = Sound, Creative Identity, Self expression-Blue

Located in the throat, this chakra is related to communication and creativity. Here we experience the world symbolically through vibration, such as language.

✓ Brow/Third Eye Chakra = Light, Archetypal Identity, Self reflection-Indigo

Located between the eye brows, this chakra is related to the act of physical and intuitive seeing. It opens our psychic faculties and understanding of archetypal levels. When healthy, this chakra allows us to see clearly - which allows us to see the 'big picture'.

✓ Crown Chakra = Thought, Universal Identity, Self knowledge-Violet

Located at the top of the head, this chakra relates to consciousness as pure awareness. It is our connection to a place of All-Knowing.   When developed, this chakra brings us knowledge, wisdom, understanding, spiritual connection and bliss.

When our chakras are balanced, our mind/body/spirit connections flow freely from one to another. This flow results in greater receptivity within our psychic mind.   In addition to just plain feeling better, we receive psychic and intuitive information that is clearer and more accurate.

The Chakras and The Laws of Attraction

In the current state of spiritual awakening, we encounter a variety of approaches to achieving self-realization and empowerment. There seem to be many options and you may find yourself moving from one alternative to another and you may even feel a sense of incompleteness and fragmentation in your spiritual life. In the emerging age of new awareness, the one significant quality of transcendence is a new understanding of the wholeness of all things-the oneness of the universe. The fragmentation we feel in our spiritual practice is in conflict with this basic principle, but the sense of divisiveness is the fault of our thinking, not the condition that actually exists. I have found that shamanism offers a unifying approach that encompasses all of the various practices in its understanding that all of the universe is one entity and that our outdated mechanistic view of fragmented parts is an artificial construct developed in humankind's effort to control his universe rather than to become a part of it. An example of this unity can be found in two seemingly disparate concepts-one from ancient times (The Chakras) and another that has received much current attention (The Laws of Attraction). It is important to understand that they are one and the same because each principle enhances the other when we practice them in harmony.

The Laws of Attraction are based on an understanding of the fields of energy that exist in and around us and offer us the opportunity to influence these fields by the attitudes and intentions that we choose. Positive thoughts attract positive energies and create realizable affirmations that enrich our lives and promote constructive changes. In the same manner, negative thoughts attract negative energies and prevent us from achieving the better opportunities that we seek. Constant attention to seeking benevolent outcomes rewards us with wonderful and munificent gifts, often beyond our greatest wishes. The Laws of Attraction make us aware that we are the masters of our fate and the determiners of our future wellbeing.

The chakras are also concerned with energy fields and are the centers of our life force in association with vital points in the physical body. Energy flows through seven centers of our body and provides healing and balance to our systems. If the chakras are blocked, one may experience illness, weakness, and disequilibrium in one's spiritual, physical, and emotional states. Focusing on positive flows of energy through the Laws of Attraction can serve to open the chakras and promote good health, security, and happiness. It bodes well for us to understand these two energy principles and to consciously exercise our bodies, minds, and spirits to attain the advantages of the wonderful energies that the universe puts at our disposal.

Each of the seven main chakras in the body has a different function in the manifestation of your reality. In their ideal state, the chakras pulse out energy that is healthy and supportive to the wellbeing of an individual. The chakras can move from an ideal state (which you are born into) to a more contaminated state throughout life. This contamination comes from life experiences and the attachments to wounds. Understanding this negatively altered condition is also the beginning of healing. First, we must understand the meaning of the individual chakras in their ideal state.

Many times the chakras close down and become contaminated with beliefs that are incongruent with their ideal state and these are felt as blocks or constrictions in the energy system. For example, if you felt as a young child that you weren't safe, you weren't secure, and that you didn't have a purpose because you were unworthy, that would be pulsed out of your root chakra. This energy then becomes part of your subtle body fields or auric fields of energy and becomes part of your broadcast energy. You then would start manifesting a reality that would support this broadcast, bringing incidences and experiences to you that would prove you aren't safe or that you are unworthy to be safe. This thinking and believing pattern sets up a cycle, which creates a reality that you come to accept and use as a motivation for your actions and decisions. The chakras are the engines of our energy broadcasts. Conforming to the Laws of Attraction, the chakras vibrate outward, engage with like energies, and draw back into our beings the energies that match our intentions. The art of healing oneself is fundamentally grounded in the understanding of our fields of energy, in the choices we make, in the intentions that we establish, and in the energies that we broadcast into our environment.

How to Use Chakra Manifestation to Awaken Your Energy

Chakra manifestation is a powerful mind skill that very few actually understand. Believe it or not, your thoughts create reality and you have the power to achieve whatever you desire. We live in a world with no limits. The only thing that can hold you back is yourself.

The greatest minds in history have known this here are some famous quotes from a few of them:

"All that we are is a result of what we have thought" - Buddha

"Whatever the mind of man can conceive, it can achieve" W. Clement Stone

"Imagination is everything. It is the preview of life's coming attractions." Albert Einstein

"What this power is, I cannot say. All I know is that it exists." Alexander Graham Bell

"You create your own universe as you go along" Winston Churchill

Here are 10 steps you can take to get started learning how to use chakra manifestation to your advantage:

1. Relax your mind, body, and soul. You must be completely relaxed to allow positive energy engulf your entire being.

2. Do away with any mind blockages, and open your spiritual mind.

3. Once you have reached an Altered Conscious State, it's time to begin the Manifestation Process.

4. Picture yourself extremely happy,completely satisfied, and feeling content.

5. Imagine that you have already achieved your goal.

6. Focus on the positive feelings of reaching your dream.

7. Use only positive words and thoughts. Avoid negative words and thoughts.

8. Linger on the good feelings, and imagine that it is really happening.

9. Speak the words and vocalize how you achieved your success.

10. Believe you already conquered your goals with all your heart.

The hardest part of all this is the first three steps. An uneasy mind can only lead to a dead end path. It can take extensive practice and intense training in meditation to learn how to change your brain waves in order to obtain the proper manifestation mindset, but attaining the proper mindset is essential for learning how to use Chakra Manifestation to it's full effect.

Chakras - How To Know If Yours Are Balanced

Chakras are energy centers within the body that affect our physical, emotional, mental and physical well-being. Chakras come from the Sanskrit word meaning "wheels of light." Chakras are like a blueprint of energy for individuality. These energy centers hold a vibration and color, like a human rainbow.

There are many ways, from yoga, meditation to mind-body techniques, that can help balance your chakras. But first, do you know if you're out of balance?

When you work on the chakras that are closed or weak, you'll be directly influencing that particular area of your life, for example, finances, sex life, self-esteem, compassion, expression, intuition and spirituality.

Are your finances in trouble? Are you feeling insecure? Do you need to perform better at work and get that raise or promotion? Strengthen your Root or 1st Chakra.

Do you want to spice up your sex life or feel more passionate and creative? Unblock your Sacral or 2nd Chakra.

Want to feel more self-confident and powerful in achieving your goals? Strengthen your Solar Plexus or 3rd Chakra.

Want to feel more love, be able to forgive past grievances, and connect better with your spouse, kids, friends and co-workers? Work on your 4th or Heart Chakra.

Afraid of public speaking? Want to be able to express your truth and be understood? Balance your 5th or Throat Chakra.

Want more inspiration on which path you should take in life? Want to increase your intuition and psychic abilities? Open your 6th or Third Eye Chakra.

Want to feel at one with all there is? Have more peace, harmony and connection to spirit? Work on your 7th or Crown Chakra.

If you want to get balanced, get centered, get energized, get relaxed, get inspired, get clear, get connected, get going... chakra healing can be your answer. When your chakras are balanced, your life will also feel balanced.

When we learn to balance our chakras, we learn to craft our lives the way we want them to be, rather than living in constant reaction to forces outside of us.

These spirals of energy are wheels that heal, feeding the body good energy and relieving it of that we do not want. Chakras cannot be held, stroked or bottled up like a genie, yet our physical bodies soak them up thirstily and they profoundly affect our metabolism, emotions, sensations and behaviors. In addition to their roles in the physical realm, chakras work on a higher plane, waking us to the realization that our body, mind and spirit are forever and inextricably linked.

If you want an "instant" healing technique for Chakra Balancing, Dynamind can hold the answer. Dynamind is the ultimate healing secret to balancing your life in just minutes a day.

Whether you experience pain, illness or stress, or just want to enhance your energy, you'll want to learn and practice this simple-yet-profound technique. Dynamind can be used to heal a wide range of dis-ease.

You simply state out loud what you want to change - the problem or pain - and tap, breathe deeply and feel the body tension causing your discomfort melt away. The concept is that by physically touching four major points on your body while reciting specific statements, you're able to take a deep breath and release tension causing disruption in your body's healing energy. It may sound simple, but the results are often deeply transformative.

Back Pain With Chakra Balance

When working with animals, it is as important to attune with them as when working with human beings. Use your intuition, your knowledge of animal body language, and the chakra system to direct your healing to the area(s) where it is most needed.

To find chakras that are unbalanced you could use a pendulum and begin to work on that chakra. There are many ways. Consider yoga postures, reiki, crystals and other forms of chakra balance. In the final article - Part 6, will be given the yoga exercises to balance the chakras and help you with your back pain.

Rubellite (dark pink) Tourmaline: Creativity, love, devotion. Unites heart and body for love, courage, passion, energy, stamina, and steadiness. High lithium content (thus pink/red colour) brings emotional balance, lovingness, devotion in a down-to-earth way. Releases reproductive Chakra blocks; stimulates fertility. Used to strengthen and detoxes blood and immune system and to ease radiation effects. Corresponds to the root and heart chakras, and the astrological signs of Sagittarius and Scorpio.

The seven chakras are located between the base of the spine and the top of the head. All body parts are represented along the chakra pathway. The first of seven chakras begins with the root chakra at the base of the spine (lower vibrations) to the Crown chakra (highest frequency/vibrations).

The higher the Chakra, the higher the vibration. Each chakra is attached to one of the seven endocrine glands of the body is represented by colour (light energy that represents specific wavelengths of light) but cannot be seen by the human eye - although people with very high spiritual perception can see people's aura's. Colour has effects on human emotion. When you are tense or irritable from daily stress, going to a room painted in lavender or pale blue will relax you- if you need energy, wear vibrant orange or red. Green is for relationships.

The Sacral Chakra is located in the lower abdomen and its' colour is orange. It governs the physical areas of the sexual organs, stomach, upper intestines, liver, gallbladder, kidney, pancreas, adrenal glands, spleen, middle spine and its associated physical disorders include lower back pain, pelvic pain, libido, prostate gland, impotence, and urinary problems. The psycho-emotional issues involved include: blame, guilt, money, sex, power, control, creativity, morality. Healthy sexuality, sensualism and emotional balance are maintained.

Using Mudras - Hand Postures - For Mind Body Spirit and Chakra Balance

Mudras have been used for many thousands of years in Eastern cultures as a way to enlightenment, mudras are still used today. Mudras are positions, typically of the hands, that influence the energies of the body, mind spirit and, directly, your chakra energy system. In addition to the hands, there are many postures in which the entire body is used.

Most readers will be familiar with the mudra held during meditation. The meditator, sitting in lotus position places both hands on one's knees while holding the tip of the thumb and first finger tip together.

Alternatively, one may place the hands on the lap with the fingers of the right hand resting on the left palm. Another form, while meditating is the "prayer position." In this position, both hands are held in front of the chest, or any chakra you want to give attention to, the palms touching.

Some mudras are performed spontaneously by many people, like the familiar Hakini mudra, where the tips of all fingers from the right hand touch the corresponding fingertips from the left.

Mudras can be used to open one's energy centers, or chakras. To heighten the effect, one may chant a specific sound for each chakra.

For all of the below, sit either in lotus position with your spine straight and your body relaxed or, sit in a chair in a comfortable position with your feet solidly touching the floor.

✓ Mudra to open your first chakra:

Let the tips of your thumb and index finger touch. Put your mind on your first chakra, between the genitals and anus. Chant the sound LAM slowly 3 times. (A = always sounds like ah)

✓ Mudra to open your second chakra:

Place your hands in your lap with your palms up, the left hand underneath, The tips of your thumbs are touching gently.

Keep your mind on your sacral bone, your tailbone. Chant VAM slowly 3 times

✓ Mudra to open your third chakra:

Place your hands in front of your belly button. Let the fingers join at the tops, pointing away from you. Cross the thumbs right over left. Keep your fingers straight. Keep your mind on your belly button and 2 inches inward. Chant the sound RAM 3 times.

✓ Mudra to open the fourth, or heart chakra:

Let the tips of your index finger and thumb touch. Place your left hand on your left knee and your right hand in front of the lower part of your breast bone above your solar plexus. Keep your mind on your heart chakra, in the middle of your chest. Chant the sound YAM 3 times.

✓ Mudra to open the 5th or throat chakra:

Make a circle with your hands, like this: Place your right hand flat and place your left fingers on top of your right fingers. Make a circle by touching the tips of your thumbs together. Pull your thumbs up a bit. Put your mind on your Adam's apple. Chant the sound HAM 3 times.

✓ Mudra to open your 6th chakra, or third eye:

Place your hands in front of your sternum, not below it, at your solar plexus, just above your solar plexus. Place your two middle fingers together facing forward and straight. The knuckles of all of your other fingers (aside from your thumbs) fold in and touch easily at the second joint counting from the top. The thumbs touch tips and point towards your sternum. Put your mind on your third eye, between and just above your eyebrows. Chant the sound OM or AUM 3 times.

✓ Mudra to open your 7th chakra or crown chakra:

Place your hands in front of your belly button. Allow the ring fingers to point up and touch at their tips. Cross the rest of your fingers, with the left thumb underneath the right. Put your mind on the top of your head. Chant the sound NG 3 times. (ING)

If you feel dizzy after opening your crown, go back and open the root again. Lie down for a while. It will go away. You just have too much energy in your higher chakras compared to your lower chakras. This is common these days. If this is the case, work on all of your chakras except to the point that you feel dizziness for 21 days and then start working up again.

Brainwave Entrainment, Ho'oponopono, and Chakra Balancing

Chakra balancing with Ho'oponopono brainwave entrainment will balance, cleanse, and activate your chakra vortexes, as you petition the Divine to release and dissolve blocks into the white light.

Brainwave entrainment is a vehicle that enhances the spiritual process of Ho'oponopono. This scientifically proven technology alters the brain's frequency by introducing specific sound patterns in a repetitive and rhythmic manner, which the brain then mimics. Access to each individual chakra frequency can be reached quickly and easily, and when combined with the mantra of Ho'oponopono, will clean and dissolve anything that is hindering their full power potential.

When your chakras are unbalanced or closed, you cannot integrate the level of consciousness that each chakra represents. Long held negative states brought on by emotional reactions and thought forms from the past, can block a chakra and can have a profound impact on your physical, emotional, mental, and spiritual health.

Your life will be out of balance.

Chakras act as gateways for light energy- a vital life force energy that enters into the physical body-- while at the same time, acting as an exit point for lower frequency energies that need to be released back into the white light of the Unified Field of Consciousness, for transmutation.

Petitioning the Divine, being in direct contact with All That Is, as each chakra is activated, using the Ho'oponopono mantra, clears, cleans and releases the negative, lower frequency that has been collected into the white light of the Unified Field of Consciousness.

Each of the seven major chakras represents a level of consciousness or developmental state of life. When these chakras are open and balanced, they form an integrated system where each depends on the other for optimal health. A blockage in one chakra, will affect all of the chakras.

How Do You Heal Your Chakras?

Healing your chakras can be done in a number of ways. You can work with them on an energetic level, a physical level, and on a holistic level. It is a matter of finding what works for you and how to use the different techniques to your advantage and what resonates within your own chakra work.

Energetic ways to heal your chakras can be a combination of using energy forms for specific chakra work, or even general based healing energy such as Usui Reiki, to heal your chakras. You can do this by running the energy, having the new energy form pool within each chakra point, and then release all negative energetic debris form the area. There are many meditations using color-guided therapies that can also correspond with using energy healing for your chakras.

Physical ways to heal your chakras can be done with simple exercises. For example, healing your crown chakra exercises would include prayer and meditation. For your root chakra simple exercises would be walking bare foot in the grass, marching, stomping your feet, and even squats.

Holistic ways to heal your chakras are about approaching the chakra point from a mind body spirit level. If it is your root chakra that needs healed, on a mind level what is important to you that deals with stability, survival issues, self-preservation, or courage. On a physical level, work on balancing these energies out through running energy and grounding. On a spirit level, make sure you connect and tap into all of the energy that is provided through Mother Earth and your spirit guides to help heal.

Chakra Balancing With Healing Stones

Each of us have an Energy body that is a very complex system. Each aura has a seemingly definite boundary and very individualistic, but at the same time one must also be aware that each energy body is actual energy, therefore, it cannot remain isolated. Our energies are constantly exposed to so many other energy bodies and are susceptible to developing cloudy, closed, and off sync chakras as a result. Healing the chakra is easy to do and can be extremely beneficial. The use of stones enhances and intensifies the healing and aligning process.

There are several stones that are appropriate for each chakra. Below are the 4 most popular crystals used for corresponding chakras:

✓ Root Chakra-Red- Grounding - Base of spine (stones can be placed at the feet as well)

1. Bloodstone- Helps alleviate anxieties that can cause unbalance in the body

Promotes detoxification thereby strengthening the kidneys, liver and spleen

2. Agate- Enhance self-esteem, assist physical and emotional security

Helpful in eliminating negativity

3. Smoky Quartz- An excellent grounding crystal that helps one focus on the present

Helpful in dissolving negative energy and emotional blockages

4. Tiger's Eye- Encourages optimism and discipline

✓ Sacral Chakra - Orange - Joy - Just below the belly button

1. Citrine- Helps develop emotional maturity

Helpful during periods of emotional instability

2. Carnelian- Helps dissolve sorrow from the emotional self

Promotes physical energy needed to take action in emotionally challenging situations

3. Moonstone- Helps in enhancing feminine side

Calms emotions to see a situation more objectively

4. Rutilated Quartz- This stone is valuable to all of the chakras for meditation, healing and spiritual development

Helps to stabilize relationships and emotional imbalances

✓ Solar Plexus - Yellow - Growth, Physical Health and Creativity - Between naval and base of sternum

1. Calcite- (Golden or yellow) Helpful with dysfunctions of the pancreas, kidneys and spleen

Helpful in "kick starting" the Solar Plexus following a clearing

2. Malachite- Helps to link the Solar Plexus to the Heart Chakra to promote the compassion necessary in preventing personal power from becoming misplaced

3. Sunstone- Known for bringing good fortune

Good for reducing stomach tension and ulcers

4. Yellow Citrine- Helps one to access their personal power and enhances self confidence

Helpful in overcoming addictions as well as digestive issues

✓ Heart Chakra - Green - Compassion and Unconditional Love - Center of chest

1. Rose Quartz- Helps one become more receptive to joys

Heals emotional wounds

2. Green Jade- Said to offer reassurance and protection to those feeling vulnerable

3. Aventurine Quartz- Excellent for depression

Encourages enthusiasm for life

4. Watermelon Tourmaline- Known as the 'super activator' of Heart Chakra and connects with Higher Self

Assists with emotional dysfunction

✓ Throat Chakra - Blue - Communication - Throat

1. Lapis Lazuli- Expands awareness and intellectual capacity

Enhances the mental clarity necessary to effectively communicate with others

2. Celestite- Can assist in clairaudience and remembering dreams

Mental clarity

3. Turquoise- Said to help one find their true path

Helpful in creative endeavors

4. Sodalite- Encourages objectivity and new perspectives, bringing harmony between the conscience and unconscience minds Clarity on how to move forward in life

✓ Third Eye Chakra - Indigo - Intuition and Wisdom - Just above and between the eyes

1. Calcite- Helps amplify the energies of the third eye

2. Purple Fluorite- Brings together rationality and intuition

Increases the ability to concentrate and strips away false illusions

3. Azurite- Helpful in stimulating the Third Eye when blocked or under utilized

4. Amethyst- A beneficial and protective energy that creates a calming influence when one is overwhelmed by intellectual and emotional turmoil

✓ Crown Chakra - Violet - Spirituality and selflessness - Top of head

1. Clear Quartz- An 'all purpose' crystal for healing that can amplify, focus and transform energy

Believed to assist Kundalini energy movement to bring about the realization spiritual power

2. Herkimer Diamond- Brings harmony of energy throughout the body

Excellent antidepressant

Promotes a desire to be rather than do

3. Amethyst- Assists in letting go and trusting

Creates a sense of spirituality and contentment

4. Diamond- Said to stimulate spirituality and keep negativity away Symbol of perfection; enables us to move toward our highest spiritual potential .

Lie on your back, keeping arms at sides and legs uncrossed. Place the stones on the appropriate chakras, beginning with the Root Chakra and ending with the Crown Chakra. Keep them on your body until your mind slows down. It's important to reach one of the slower brain wave states so that your body is receptive to the healing process, however do not fall asleep. If you are one who meditates regularly or have some experience doing so, meditate with the stones on your chakras for at least 15 minutes. If meditation is new to you, you may find that listening to a CD with guided meditation makes it very easy for the novice.

When you have finished your meditation with the stones, be sure to cleanse your stones. They will absorb unwanted energy and need to be cleaned.

There is more than one method for achieving this but the simplest way is to use sea salt. Salt can be mixed with water or use it dry. When using salt water, combine a tablespoon of sea salt in a glass or ceramic mug of cold water. Do not use metal or plastic containers. Place the stones in the solution and allow to soak overnight. To use dry salt, place the sea salt in a glass or non-plastic container and bury the crystals with the points facing downward into the salt. Again, leave overnight. Sometimes a stone may take longer to clear, especially if it has been used in a deep, intense healing. If this is the case, leave another day or two in the sea salt. When clearing gemstone necklaces it is best to use the dry sea salt method. Make sure you are only using sea salt, not table salt. Table salt contains aluminum and other chemicals.

Another easy method is to use some white sage and burn it until a good strong smoke is coming from your sage. Hold the stone in this smoke for at least one minute, ideally three or four minutes.

Kyanite - The Chakra Alignment Stone

Kyanite isn't the most attractive stone to be found in your local crystal shop but it is one of the most active crystals. If it wasn't for the blue hue it could be mistaken for a piece of rough slate and passed over without much thought. However, this stone has one or two qualities that make it stand out from the hoards of other crystals you may wish to buy.

Kyanite never needs cleansing of negative influences and energies. There are one or two other crystals with this property that I am aware of (Citrine being another) as opposed to the majority of stones available. No need to run it under water and recharge in the rays of the sun for this little gem (pun intended). It vibrates very highly and is always ready for use. You could quite possibly wander through the very fires of hell and (so long as it didn't melt) your Kyanite stone would still be as pure as it was when it was first formed.

✓ Chakra Alignment Made Easy

The other hugely beneficial advantage of this stone is that it automatically aligns your chakras. You don't have to do anything other than hold a piece for a second or so and they snick back into place instantly. This can be quite disconcerting, if you are sensitive enough to feel it, especially if it's the first time you pick up a piece and were not expecting it. I feel it as if there is a gentle energetic beam running from my crown, straight down through my body and out between my legs.

This property, and it's high vibrational rate, makes it an ideal accompaniment for meditation should you wish to access 'higher realms', investigate your third eye or other upper chakra activities. Due to its high energy it isn't quite so suitable for the more relaxing meditation practices, but having your Chakras aligned whilst relaxing is always an advantage so I leave the decision when to use it up to you.

✓ Crystal Healing

Some may think that this stone could prove to be the end of a large part of the Crystal Healing business but I don't believe this to be the case. Having experienced the strength of Kyanite myself whilst I was in a severely unbalanced energetic state, I can safely say that this stone could prove to be too strong for some people. It was initially quite uncomfortable to hold for more than a few minutes, and it took a good couple of weeks for me to be able to tolerate the stone for any longer. If someone of a nervous disposition tried this themselves then they could be put off crystal therapy altogether.

How to Balance Your Root or Base Chakra

Are you struggling with your entire frame of mind, which seems to be spacey and disorganized? Are you readily controlled by strong feelings of anger over simple things? Do you feel your confidence and drive has been thrown out of the window, and you can't focus on your goals anymore? Chances are you seriously need root chakra balancing to restore back the lost confidence in place of fear, calm in place of anger, and drive in place of pessimism. Chakras, especially the root chakra, are stunning yet somewhat complicated. The base chakra is the ultimate foundation of other chakra, and if it's unbalanced, then other chakras will follow suit.

How do you balance your base or root chakra? First and foremost, envision the red color glowing at the end of your spinal cord, where this energy center is located. Starting with simple meditation, you have to picture a bright red light at the base of your spinal Cord. This is the ultimate beginning of cleansing and balancing your base chakra. Another stunning way to balance this chakra is by dancing. If you are not a good and passionate dancer, then this is the perfect opportunity to better your dancing skills and the physical activity is an excellent way to release endorphins and collect feel-good energy. Better still sing along to the music you are dancing to as this helps balance your throat chakra as well.

Yoga is an incredible solution when you want to balance any chakra, even your base chakra. There are quite a number of yoga postures that are ultimate for the root chakra's cleansing and balancing. Some of these yoga poses, like the tree posture, go hand in hand with the red visualization procedure. The tree pose is exceedingly helpful in balancing the base chakra, particularly if you concentrate on this meditation and form the tree pose single handedly. Ensure you feel sufficiently connected to the earth when performing this yoga pose, and don't forget to engage your core.

Surprisingly, taking a shower is an incredible base chakra cleaner. It is significant to love and fully embrace your physical being by taking a shower. Bathing mindfully is a superb form of meditation, particularly for your root chakra. After a satisfactory shower, a walk outside can enhance the balancing of your base chakra. Taking a mindful walk while concentrating deeply on every step you make will give this energy center a fantastic chance to cleanse itself. Moreover, paying attention to every step you take gives your mind a break from disruptive thoughts or issues that may be causing stress and allowing your base chakra to balance.

As with all of the seven major chakras, imbalanced and blockages are various and in some circumstances an individual may benefit from chakra balancing sessions with an experienced energy healer. There are also professional Reiki Masters and even courses available on virtual platforms to educate and provide free resources to those interested in maintaining their chakras. In many cases, an imbalance of blockage of the root chakra can spread or impact the function of other energy centers and gifted psychic advisors may be able to assist in identifying underlying factors associated with the chakra system when the individual suffering from the imbalance wouldn't have known the source of their dysfunction otherwise, which often leads to a worsened condition.

Getting a heart filling massage can be the perfect solution to balancing your base chakra. Feeling good about your physical self can bring back the lost confidence and drive. Exploring and realizing the beauty of our physical selves can help clear out incriminating feeling of anger and fear that causes insecurity and other feelings of adversity caused by such variations of an imbalanced base chakra, hence balancing the energy center all together. Balancing the root chakra is just like building a strong foundation for your house. Keep the root chakra balanced, and sure enough, you will have a healthy, balanced, open chakra system.

How to Balance Your Sacral Chakra

The sacral chakra is primarily located in the lower abdomen, approximately two-inches below the navel system. Have you met an individual who for some reason radiates warmth and friendliness with a tendency to be abnormally attached? Well, this is the renowned sign of sacral chakra imbalance of excess. Other manifestations of such an imbalance include timidity, hypersensitivity, sexuality issues, trust issues and emotional volatility. This energy center determines a person's emotional connectivity and relations to other individuals. Undoubtedly, every individual will experience imbalance within the sacral chakra at least once in their lifetime. Consequently, learning how to balance this is quite beneficial in maintaining your emotional and mental health. Doing so can bring tremendous improvement in overall wellbeing.

Balancing this energy center is like balancing other chakras; it resonates with a specific color and sound. This chakra's relieving color is orange. Imagine a bright healing orange color glowing on your entire lower abdomen, focusing utterly on your breath and releasing any stresses. This helps significantly in balancing your sacral chakra, eliminating any sort of tension or disease. The other balancing option is to dance to an insane level, like no one is watching. This has been proven as one of the easiest and best balancing techniques. By dancing your hips off, you will be cleansing and balancing this energy center and gaining from the physical exercise.

There is always some physical tension and emotional baggage in the hips that is why there are numerous hip opening yoga poses. The sacral chakra is directly connected to your lower abdomen and your hips. Focusing on some notable hip opening yoga postures can help substantially in balancing this chakra as well. Although there are numerous hip opening yoga postures, it is convenient to focus on a few postures, practicing them on a daily basis until you utterly attain the desired sacral chakra balance. This can take time and patience but will have a very rewarding outcome.

While hip opening yoga poses can do a terrific sacral chakra balancing job, toning up will make the results even better. Keeping your body fit releases undesirable physical and emotional tension, entirely cleansing up this energy center. Furthermore, reliable tone-up exercises prepare the physical and emotional self for meditation. Balancing all the other chakras is key in the balancing of the sacral chakra. Considering one chakra imbalance often manifests imbalances in all other chakras-especially the sacral upon the thought due to direct connection--it is imperative that individuals wishing to pursue a greater control over their emotional and physical wellbeing take alignment into account. In meditation sessions, try to relieve all the chakras of undesirable physical and mental tension.

Learning and trying to let go of emotional and mental baggage in your life is also instrumental in balancing your sacral chakra. There are gifted psychics that can see into your spiritual anatomy and help you with identifying problematic energy centers and coaching on how to maintain and balanee these centers. It is critical to let go of undesirable tension and welcome new, enthralling things into your life. In life, there are many emotional situations that we get intertwined in. If you are intertwined in any emotional baggage, then it's time to relieve yourself of this tension. There with the capability to identify problematic areas in terms of imbalance in energy centers and what other chakras may be affected by the imbalance and offer coaching or assistance in chakra balancing sessions. Maintaining a balanced sacral chakra will open a new, fantastic emotional world to you. Cleansing and balancing your sacral chakra will restore the zest of life, renew your ultimate life goals and will help balance your overall emotional self.

How to Balance Your Throat Chakra

The throat chakra is undeniably the communication center of the body, and as such, it plays a significant role in creativity, effective communication and expression; which are essential in productivity and harmonized relationships. An imbalanced throat chakra can manifest concerns including talking too much, fear, and arrogance, being manipulative and deceit. On the other hand, there are many benefits to this energy center being well-balanced. Benefits include excellent communication and expression skills of oneself, which don't have to be necessarily verbal. Artistic contentment and harmony are also non-verbal benefits as well as a plethora of other positives..

Your ears and shoulders are somewhat connected to this energy center and any imbalance in this chakra can stir concrete problems in these areas. Not only will an imbalance in this center cause the adverse reactions listed above, it can also be as a result of physical, emotional and mental issues. Having an infection in your throat also results in an imbalance but is usually easily corrected without any extensive intervention. Balancing this chakra is not at all complicated, anyone can do it! With some straightforward activities, you can be able to balance your throat chakra, restoring effective communication and desirable artistic expression in your life.

The ultimate and particularly renowned way to balance the throat chakra is by singing. Even if you posses a less than intriguing voice, putting some favorite songs and singing along will help cleanse and balance your throat chakra. Better still, you can dance along those songs to balance your base chakra as well. Drinking water is such a simple way to cleanse and balance your throat chakra. Extremely simple exercises and daily task contribute to the overall balance such as; humming, drinking water, and singing are a few simple, yet effective exercise. More importantly, you have to control what you ingest from time to time as this helps balance this energy center and as with all chakras there are foods that resonate specifically with each one.

An imbalanced throat can be a direct effect of the emotional baggage you store at your hips. Consequently, next time you get on your yoga mat, try some deep hip opening poses. While performing these poses, you should also pay attention to your throat, releasing any stress. Often at times, chakras are stimulated by a specific color. The color blue resonates with the throat chakra. Another balancing technique is to visualize a beautiful blue light at the core of your throat. With the blue color envisioned in your throat, you can inhale and exhale softly, each time trying to release the stress in your throat.

A good neck and shoulder massage can be instrumental in relieving your throat of any stress, helping you to maintain balance. The throat balancing power of a wonderful neck and shoulder massage is incomparable to any other. Speaking the ultimate truth at all times ensures your throat chakra health. The truth speaking mantra always balances the throat chakra. Balancing the throat chakra is a heavenly practice to improve communication with fellow human beings and with the higher divine energy. Balance your throat chakra, and you will be utterly surprised at how better your communication and non-verbal expression will become and how harmonious your relationships may become .

The Crown Chakra - Healing & Balancing the Seventh Chakra

The crown, or seventh chakra, is situated at the crown of the head. This article takes a look at the characteristics of this chakra, and the importance of keeping it in balance.

This chakra is also known as the 'thousand-petalled lotus', as well as 'Sahasrara' in traditional Sanskrit terminology. It is associated with the colours white and violet, and connects the individual with the larger spiritual self. A balanced seventh chakra fosters a sense of cosmic unity and oneness, as well as a powerful sense of intuition. In terms of its influence on the physical body, it is associated with the top of the head area and the pineal gland.

Imbalances in the crown chakra often manifest as depression, an apathetic attitude, and a sense of social isolation and inability to connect with others.

✓ Balancing The Crown Chakra

The seventh chakra can be rebalanced using various methods, such as crystal healing. It is particularly responsive to diamonds, although clear crystal quartz also works very well, and either can be placed in the crown area as part of a crystal healing session.

The use of a crown chakra meditation can also be very beneficial. Traditional chakra meditations often involve using guided imagery, although modern technology has made these more effective and easier to use for those who aren't used to meditation, thanks to brainwave entrainment.

If you use a brainwave entrainment recording for tuning the crown chakra, you'll hear sounds of specific frequencies which have been found to have a direct and beneficial influence on this energy centre. Like every other part of the mind-body complex, each chakra is associated with a specific frequency when functioning optimally, and exposure to sounds of the correct frequencies can help bring the chakra into balance with relatively little effort on your part.

To use this method, you should be prepared to set aside some time each day to listen to your recording in a quiet place where you won't be disturbed. Although many people get great results right away, this isn't always the case, so it's important to be consistent and listen regularly. With some time and regular use, a chakra balancing meditation recording can have a very beneficial effect on the health of your crown chakra.

30 Benefits of Clearing and Balancing Your Chakras

Do You pay attention to your chakras? They're there working in balance or out of balance all the time whether You pay attention or not. Why not tap into the healing potential available to You by being conscious about your chakra energetic system?

Do you ever have physical, emotional or mental issues that just don't ever seem to be resolved or keep reoccurring? Chakra imbalances can show up in various ways. Here is a list of some common manifestations of chakras not functioning properly. Do You recognize any of these symptoms?

- Physical Imbalances
- Low back pain
- Repeated injury to the same area
- Bladder or bowel issues
- Skin disorders
- Immune disorders

- Lack of Circulation
- Reproductive disorders
- Low sex drive
- Digestive disorders
- Thyroid problems
- Heart Disorders
- TMJ
- Dental issues
- Eye weakness
- Breathing Issues
- Headaches
- Nervous disorders
- Emotional Imbalances
- Low self Esteem
- Need for Approval
- Eating disorders
- Inability to express self
- Lack of willpower
- Abusiveness, self or others
- Anger
- Deep Sadness
- Close hearted
- Moodiness
- Addictions
- Depression
- Mental Imbalances

- Jealousy
- Resentment
- Indecision
- Unclear communicating
- Boredom and Apathy
- Judgement
- Criticism
- Lack of Creativity
- Overly analytical
- Dogmatic
- Materialistic
- Ego centered
- Lack of Motivation
- Disconnected to life reality
- Exclusion
- Scattered
- Unstable
- Insecure
- Fear of Lack

You can learn to be aware of your chakras and harmonize and balance the energy running through them. By clearing your chakras you may experience the following benefits:

30 Benefits of clearing and balancing chakras

- Increased awareness and openness to Psychic and Spiritual Information
- Faster and greater ability to heal your Physical, Emotional, Mental and Spiritual Issues
- Transform weaknesses into strengths
- Easier Release of Non Supportive Patterns
- Increased Passion for Life
- Experience the Power of living Present in the Now
- Overcome boredom by infusing spirit into mundane
- Become comfortable facing uncertainty by tapping into the stability of your Self
- Increased manifesting ability to create what You want in life
- Access financial wisdom
- Enjoy healthy and loving relationships
- Greater pleasure and enjoyment in life
- Realization of your self worth

- Make clear choices that reflect who You are
- Self confidence to accept and express yourself
- Ease in experiencing Love and forgiveness of self and others.
- Access inspiration to turn dreams into reality
- Awareness and dedication to your Highest life path.
- Increase the health and strength of your immune system
- Recognition and increase intuition
- Express and release emotions in a healthy manner
- Increased personal integrity
- Attain self mastery
- Access your inner wisdom
- Enjoy the clarity of a focused mind
- Abundant inner guidance by maintaining a strong connection to Source
- Live your Highest Life Path
- Tap into your Will Power
- Clear communication of your heart and mind

-    Experience the power of being grounded in physical and your Spiritual Higher Self simultaneously

-    The benefits of clear and healthy functioning chakras are available to anyone. With easy to learn techniques and meditations your understanding and conscious awareness of your chakras can propel you into living the life you deserve to live.

Balancing Your Chakras to Heal Emotional Eating

Energy Balancing of the Chakras, when combined with hypnosis, can help a person lose weight and feed the "Hungry Heart" of emotional eating. I have noticed many overweight people are "leaking" energy in what I named the "Hunger Chakra" located in the "basin" of the lower stomach, also known as the Sacral Chakra area. If you are challenged with the frustrations of excess weight and "yo-yo" dieting, ask yourself these questions:

- Are you always Hungry?
- Have you tried everything to lose weight?
- Have you wasted enough of your precious time, energy and money on this weight release problem?

If you answered yes to any of these questions, then perhaps you need to go deeper beneath the layers of the weight loss puzzle to find a missing piece....Chakra Balancing.

Knowledge of the Chakras is ancient and new scientific research gives credence to this theory. The ancient Hindus specified that we have 7 Sacred Energy centers running from the base of your spine to the top of your head which correspond to certain bodily organ functions, psychological functions, emotional and spiritual centers. Their interconnected balance plays a profound role in every aspect of your life and well being. According to recent scientific studies, each Chakra location corresponds with a major bundle of nerves beginning at the base of your spine and ending at the brain's cerebral cortex. If any Chakra is blocked or imbalanced due to fear, stress, negative programming or inactivity, then your overall well being is affected. You can even sense a deficiency or imbalance in that area if it feels constricted or cold/hot or you feel stress or pain in that area.

Your Sacral Chakra is located in the sacral region of your body about two inches down from your navel to your pelvic area. The Sacral Chakra is "the seat" or the origin of our instinctual cravings, desires and habitual responses-and is intimately connected to emotional eating. Desires, impulses and cravings rule the Sacral Chakra. They are for food, sex, relationships and procreating. This is also where the instinctual "Hungry Beast" resides, the part of your subconscious mind that just wants to be gratified and feed all the time. So how do you quiet the "Hungry Beast" whose voracious appetite constantly demands to be fed? In order to "tame" the Hungry Beast, there are learned bad habits, learned behaviors and an unhealthy lifestyle to address; as well as the issue of emotional eating used to medicate, sooth or repress emotions. Digging even deeper, there is the Spiritual Hunger that yearns to be feed to fill the "hole in the soul" that no food will ever fill!

The mind and will power exerted to "beat" the Hungry Beast into submission through strict diets and deprivation, don't work in the long run. It is human nature to desire what we are deprived of-setting most up for a binge. Your body is wired to seek energy when it is starving. To fulfill that Spiritual Hunger however, your Heart Chakra, located in the center of your chest is the great healer and transformer and balancer of all the Chakras. Only through the wisdom of your Heart Chakra, working in concert with your "Hungry" Sacral Chakra, the need to achieve Balance can help to tame the Hungry Beast.

Listen with your Heart Chakra! Treat your body as your own best friend-with respect, care and compassion. Listen to your body's needs and messages to you. Ask your body: What do you need? What kinds of food do you need to fuel well to feel well? Are you really hungry-or do you need to be nourished and comforted by love and kindness-reaching out to a loved one-or to extend love or a helping hand to another? Do you need to move and stretch your body? Do you need to take in a deep delicious breath? Or are you starving for some "me" time? A very simple exercise to Balance your Hungry Sacral Chakra is to connect with the healing and transformative energy of the sacred Heart Chakra. The Technique is as follows:

First rub your hands together and place one of your hands your sacral area about two inches down from your navel and your other hand over your heart. You can easily "connect" with your chakras through your life breath.....just follow the flow of breath moving in and out as you release, relax and let go into your body as you imagine your breath is just like the flow of the ocean waves. Imagine the gentle flow of a radiant breath of light moving in and out through the center of your heart. Feel, sense or imagine there is an eternal flame of light within the center of your heart-the light of your soul. Feel this inner light grow brighter and more radiant-opening up and filling all the dark spaces and places within you and illuminating your life with love, forgiveness, peace and understanding. You can even allow your love light to grow brighter as you bring to mind a loved one, the smile of a baby, giggles of children playing, a treasured pet, a beautiful sunset or a scene in nature that takes your breath away!..Just stay a moment here.

Now imagine a cord of spiraling light connecting from your Heart Chakra to your Sacral Chakra and the cord of light spirals up from your sacral chakra and one that spirals down from your heart chakra intertwining like a double helix of spiraling light. The balancing color of your Sacral Chakra is orange. As you are inhaling and exhaling, imagine a golden orange ball of light warming your belly area and filling it with light. Allow its orange glowing radiance to glow brighter and brighter. Feel the light filling any empty spaces and places within your belly with the warmth and radiance of the sun.

Imagine this area as an open vessel, a bowl of light that opens and receives this good positive energy and becomes revitalized and recharged and full. Take in as much as you need to take in and feels good to you. Now rotate your hands first in a clockwise and then counterclockwise position 7x to balance and anchor this energy within your body. Next, check in with your body and ask what it really needs....Listen to your body. Now repeat the following affirmations out loud:

✓ I am connected to my Divine/Source energy

✓ I am loving and compassionate

✓ I appreciate my body and treat it with respect

✓ I draw in vitality

✓ I honor my body and its needs.

✓ I feel my emotions and I am connected to my center of well being,

✓ I honor my emotions as they are my internal guide.

✓ I reach out to the world in healthy ways

✓ I am nourished by healthy relationships

✓ I establish healthy boundaries.

✓ I have a healthy relationship to my body and to food.

✓ I am grateful.

✓ I honor and appreciate the energies of these chakras in my life. I am connected to Source/Divine energy.

✓ I radiate good health and wellbeing.

Physical And Spiritual Attributes Of The Third Eye Chakra

Many people have heard of the "third eye" but have no idea what this actually means.

The term third eye refers specifically to the third eye (or brow) chakra, or the sixth major energetic chakra. It is located approximately in the center of the eyebrows, between and above the two physical eyes. In Sanskrit this chakra is called ajna and the color associated with it is indigo.

The third eye is associated with actual physical vision, and when it is out of balance (either overactive or underactive) there may be disturbances in an individual's eyesight or in the eye area generally, as well as issues concerning the sinuses, nose, brain and face. Spiritually there may be an overabundance of unwanted psychic seeing and knowing; that is, the seeing of spirits, sensing of energies, presence of psychic or paranormal phenomena, etc. (Note: for many psychics and spiritual adepts, there is no overabundance of these types of things -overabundance indicates "too much" of something, yet once truly spiritually and psychically developed, all phenomena is placed in its proper context, managed appropriately and, essentially, appreciated.)

Spiritually this chakra is associated with psychic seeing and intuition, and when meditated upon -- a variety of methods are available -- it can be opened and strengthened, increasing a person's natural (or supernatural, if you will) psychic gifts, including but not limited to the main psychic "clairs", those being clairvoyance, clairaudience, clairsentience, claircognizance, clairaliance and clairgustance. It is through this ajna or third eye chakra that individuals psychically perceive, be it energies, spirits, or subtle shifts in the psychic or spiritual environments.

A common occurrence originating within the third eye is what Muktananda and others referred to as "the blue pearl". It is a (typically) tiny blue/indigo dot occurring within a person's actual range of vision. Personally, on average I do see these energetic dots as blue, but sometimes they appear as gold or white --- there is no hard and fast rule. When these points of light are observed it usually indicates that the third eye is in fact opening or opened; in my experience it may also indicate the presence of an actual spiritual being (ghost) or force (guide, angel, etc.), which would be uncommon to see without an opened or awakened third eye.

Emotionally, when the third eye chakra is out of balance a person lacks insight and sound perception. They do not see clearly, whether pertaining to the inner or outer things, and this may render them confused, disoriented and even aggressive. Physically, when this chakra is out of balance, an individual might experience headaches, brain fog, brain tumors, faulty memory, sinus maladies and more.

When the third eye chakra is balanced and healthy an individual will be able to accurately intuit details about their environment, conditions, people encountered and even future events. Psychic phenomena around a person will also increase commensurate to the awakening and full functioning of the third eye.

Therefore if you are actively interested in developing psychically and spiritually, you should cultivate a keen interest in the energetic chakra system generally, and specifically as it concerns the third eye chakra.

Chakras and Tantric Yoga

Chakras are the energy centers parallel to the spine. According to Yogic Philosophy there are considered to be 7 Chakras. The Chakras vibrate at different frequencies and each Chakra is associated with a certain power and attribute that improves our experience and existence: Muladhara (root) - Root, Syashisthana (sweetness) - Sensual, Manipura (lustrous gem) -Power, Anahata (love) - Love, Vishuddha (purification) - Communication, Ajna (to perceive) - Perception and Sahasrara (thousand petalled) - Universal Connection.

There are different ways to tune into the energy centers for stimulating and strengthening each Chakra. Tuning into this energy will enable us to deal with the specific life challenges of each energy center or chakra and as a consequence to live more enhanced, meaningful and stress free lives. Yoga defines exercises and postures that help our bodies harmonize and balance the energy centers.

Tantric Yoga teaches the tools and techniques for achieving the required balance through refinement of thoughts, breathing exercises (Pranayama), contemplation, visualization and repetitive chanting of mantras, and meditation.

Tantric Yoga offers us the ways to identify and cleanse the thoughts and feelings. Using these practices to refine our thoughts and feelings we can acquire the ability to control them. The first step towards this is to identify the factors influencing our thoughts and feelings as occurring due to ignorance and materialistic attachments.

The next tool is breathing (Pranayama) and other exercises (called mudras and asanas) prescribed by Tantric Yoga. The exercises will help regulate the flow of life energy which is required for maintaining a healthy immune system and balanced emotional state. The exercises energize the body and help regulate the flow of energy.

Visualization is the perception of the symbolic representations (yantras) and deities, which serve as centering devices for the energy centers and in Meditation. The mantras include the Seed Syllables (Bija Mantras). The sound of each syllable representing each Chakra. Chanting of these syllables will bring in harmony into the chakras or energy system.

Meditation is attaining a deeper state of consciousness. Tantric Yoga teaches methods for meditation, with the use of visualization and/or mantra chanting techniques to attain meditative state.

The balancing of the Chakras and Tantric Yoga will help us control our feelings and lead to a happy, peaceful and content state of mind.

Balance Your Chakras Through Reiki Self Attunement - 3 Free Exercises

Light, Love, and Intelligence are the essence of pure energy. Your thoughts control the energy flow within and around you. Different energy centers within and around your body are influenced by your thinking habits. In other words, the things you concentrate on the most, - money, spirituality, relationships, and so on - affect your energy centers. These energy centers are known as your chakras and you can balance these Chakras through Reiki Self Attunement.

Discussed are 3 free exercises to balance your chakras through Reiki and visualization.

1. The White Light:

In your mind's eye, see a large beam of bright, crystal - white light coming into the top of your head. Make this light as bright as you can imagine. See and feel the light penetrating the inside of the top of your head, clearing away any darkness and negative thoughts from your crown chakra. Let the light travel through your body and imagine it clearing away all darkness throughout all the chakras. At the end of this meditation, you should be able to imagine all your chakras illuminated and perfectly balanced in size.

2. Breathing Colors:

As you take a deep breath, visualize yourself breathing in the color green. As you exhale completely, see yourself breathing out the color yellow. Next, breathe in the color blue as deeply as you can, and breathe out the color orange. Then, draw in the color purple with your breath, seeing the purple entering all of your cells and your blood stream. Finally, breathe out the color red completely. Repeat this meditation process three times.

3. Glass Globes:

Visualize eight beautiful glass globes stacked on top of one another. The globes are stacked from top to bottom: Royal-Purple, Red-Violet, Deep Blue, Sky Blue,

Emerald Green, Sunshine Yellow, Vivid Orange, and Ruby Red. See the globes become larger, brighter, and increasingly illuminated with light. Make them all grow in size until they are equally large. See the globes as perfectly transparent and the colors as clear, without any spots on the glass.

These 3 exercises are great for beginners who are looking to balance their chakras. Reiki self attunement can help one learn better meditation, clear and balance chakras, and heal with energy any time of day.

How the Chakras Affect Our Personality and How to Clear and Balance Them

The focus of this article will be on what aspect of your personality the different chakras relate to and two easy techniques to clear and balance them. Its important that the energy centers are clear and aligned, since that allows the energy to flow freely up and down the spine and throughout the nervous system. The result is often a feeling of peace and a sense of well-being because the physical, mental, emotional and spiritual bodies are directly related to the chakra system. Tension, negative emotions and other unbalanced energies can be released from the chakras, which can help the person as a whole, since there is a connection between all the bodies. Because the chakras are all connected, when one area is worked with the entire chakra system is affected.

✓ Qualities of the Chakras

First Chakra-Red: Some of its qualities are motivation, passion, strength and grounding. Red helps to give us vitality, courage, inner strength and self-confidence, and encourages us to achieve our goals. It gives us the power and strength to pursue our dreams.

Second Chakra-Orange: It is connected to our emotional and feeling self, and some of its qualities are joy, happiness and being sociable.

Third Chakra-Yellow: This is our ego center and some of its qualities are optimism, intelligence and being mentally creative. The heart is greatly affected by this chakra.

Fourth Chakra-Green: The Solar Plexus Chakra is an energy clearing house center. It is believed that a large portion of energy from the lower chakras pass through this front chakra before reaching the higher chakras and vice versa. The whole body can be strengthened by energizing this chakra. This chakra is connected to our loving self. Some of its qualities are harmony, kindness, sensitivity, emotional balancing, unconditional love, understanding and growth.

Fifth Chakra-Blue: The Throat Chakra is connected to our expressive self. Some of its qualities are honesty, politeness, creative self-expression and will. It also helps with detailed planning and organizing.

Sixth Chakra-Indigo: This chakra is also called the master chakra because it directs and controls the other chakras and their corresponding endocrine glands. It is also called the third eye, since it's connected to our universal seeing self. Some of the qualities are wisdom, truth seeking and intuition.

Seventh Chakra-Violet: This chakra is connected to our knowing and spiritual self. Some of the qualities are inspiration, charisma, ability to see the beauty in life, and it helps to purify thoughts and feelings. It increases our artistic and creative abilities as well.

There are many techniques for clearing, balancing and energizing the chakras, but I'll give you a couple of simple ones that anyone can do. First Technique: Shake your hands to clear old energy, then, rub your hands briskly together. This activates the minor chakras in your hands and gets the energy moving. They may feel warm. Next, put both hands over the chakra you want to work with. Imagine Universal healing energy coming into your hands as you give the intent to clear, balance and energize the chakra you have your hands on. You may feel heat going into that area as this happens. Continue for a couple of minutes or until you feel it is done. Shake off the energy when you're through. Repeat the procedure for the next chakra.

Second Technique: This one might be easier if you lie down. Shake your hands to clear the energy, then, rub them briskly together. Next, open both hands, palms down, with one on top of the other. Place both hands over the chakra you are working with and begin circling counterclockwise about 3 to 4 inches above the chakra. Make slow counterclockwise circles over the chakra for approximately one to two minutes or until you feel it is complete.

Next shake your hands to clear the energy and circle clockwise for half as long as the counterclockwise direction. The clockwise direction soothes and stabilizes the cleared chakra. Repeat the same process for each chakra that you are clearing. For a man, clear the crown chakra clockwise to clear and then counterclockwise to sooth. All the other chakras are the same as described above.

You can use these techniques daily or whenever you feel the need. Begin with an area where you are feeling discomfort. Each chakra has its own personality traits as described above. Look at the specific areas that are causing you discomfort, such as the heart chakra. This process may bring up toxic or blocked energies which will then be able to move out of your body. Since we express ourselves through these energy centers, once cleared of tension and negative emotions, we can move into a more balanced state of well-being. Remember that the chakras are all connected, so clearing one will impact the others as well. Clearing the chakras will boost your entire energy system.

Top Chakra Cleansing and Chakra Clearing Methods

Chakras are the prime forces of our body. Sometimes proper methods of chakra cleansing and chakra clearing must be used. There must be a concord between the chakras so as to make the body perform it functions in a proper manner. Chakras are greatly influenced not only by the physical and chemical factors of the environment but also by the changes within the body.

They are the energy centers and they are the ones that give balance to our body. They are also vital for the mental and physical activities and therefore it has to be purified. Right from olden days many methods are used for chakra clearing. Some of the common chakra cleansing methods are:

* There are certain aromatic substances like incense sticks and herbs and when they are burnt they give rise to fragrance.

They have the power to prevent negative energies entering our body. So this has been a common method used for cleaning chakras right from the olden days.

* Auric method is another commonly followed method of cleansing chakras where certain gems and crystals are used for the same. A disadvantage of this method is that instead of cleansing it may cause harm. So it must be consulted with trained professionals before performing this activity.

*If an individual has a balanced diet with plenty of water regularly there is a possibility of cleansing the chakras. *In addition to our balanced diet if an individual takes fresh juice and sleeps at least for eight hours a day the chakras would be cleaned to a greater extent.

*For the proper functioning of the heart and cleansing the chakras regular exercise is a must. *Nature is another source to cleanse our chakras. So if an individual spends his time in the morning sunlight and evening breeze his chakras would be cleaned.

*Listening to music makes our mind light and it refreshes our chakras.

*Meditation has the supreme power to control our senses and therefore increases the strength of our Chakras. Chakra meditation will help you improve focus. One great addition to meditation is adding bianural beats while meditating.

*Apart from all this an individual should love himself. This would give him self confidence and provoke him to lead a better life.

*One should have control over his emotions and feelings. This helps to maintain our chakras and energy levels.

Following all these habits may be difficult. But one should follow at least what they could in order to keep their mind and body peaceful

Symptoms of Malfunctioning Chakras

People today often find themselves drained or blocked in various areas of their lives. Trying to find relief, they eat differently, take medication, go into therapy, but often find no relief. But what if they discovered there was another cause for their problems that could be easily solved, sometimes by themselves, or with the help of a trained guide? How much lost potential could be restored to individual lives and how would that improve society as a whole?

The cause for untreatable problems may well lie in the chakras- the energy centers of the body which generate and allow the flow of vitality through one's physical, mental and spiritual being. Ask yourself the following questions. Any 'Yes' answers could indicate a malfunction in the chakras.

- Do I feel physically drained, lacking and stifled in energy?

- Are my relationships impaired by my emotional reactions?

- Are my will-power and self-esteem suffering, causing me to lose the battle against addictive and unhealthy behaviors?

- Am I hampered in feeling and showing the care and compassion I should to the good, positive, and dependent people in my life?

- Am I unable to express myself clearly to others and/or suffering from blockages in my creative abilities?

- Are my perceptions of reality skewed or confused? Is my thinking unclear?

- Am I unrealistically pessimistic or optimistic?

- Do I find it difficult or uninteresting to relate to the higher aspects of life, finding and creating meaning, trusting and aspiring to find and develop the best in myself, in others and in life in general?

If you find yourself struggling in any of these areas, you may well require assistance in unblocking and strengthening your chakras.

How to Open the Heart Chakra

The heart chakra located at the center of the chest, is the chakra of compassion and love. Your ability handling issues of love, grief, hatred, anger, jealousy, fears of betrayal, and loneliness depends on the condition of your heart chakra. You will find that if you open your heart chakra, handling these issues in a positive way will come more naturally to you. A popular technique often used for exercising our heart energy, is through mantra meditation. Each chakra has a specific sound or "mantra", by reciting the heart chakra's mantra you will effectively be able to open the chakra point, effectively stimulating and strengthening it in the process.

If you happen to have a mala, which is a special string of beads used for counting mantra recitations you can use it for this exercise. If you don't that's okay, you can just count the recitations in your head instead.

Before we proceed with the exercise, I would like to forewarn you that this is a serious technique that will generate a large flow of energy. Please be careful not to overdo it, over stimulation of the heart chakra can lead to an imbalance of the other chakras. This technique should only be used in addition with other techniques that will prepare you body to handle this new energy.

Now without any further delay, here are my guidelines to performing this mantra meditation.

1.Find a quiet and comfortable place to sit down on the floor cross legged.

2. Close your eyes, and recite the heart chakra's mantra which is "YAM".

3. As you are chanting this visualize and focus on your heart chakra at the center of your chest.

If chanted correctly, you will notice a new rush of energy. For beginners, I recommend that you do not exceed more than 20 recitations per session.

Yoga in Practice: Ajna Chakra

Chakras are vortices located in the subtle body. Ajna chakra is located between the eyebrows. The existence of chakras is a point of contention to some. Yogis, and Yoginis, may practice balancing their chakras, while some religious fundamentalists feel this practice borders on witchcraft. However, let's discuss one chakra that most everyone can identify with.

Ajna chakra is referred to as the "third eye" and is sometimes called,"the mind's eye." Whether you believe in the existence of chakras, or not, most of us accept the concepts of intuition and insight. These concepts enable us to use self-reflection for our own advancement.

Most Yoga practitioners think only in terms of physical Yoga (Hatha Yoga), only. Yet all Yoga practitioners are aware that Yoga involves physical, mental, and spiritual aspects. Therefore, let's use the "window of your mind" to your advantage. Visualization is commonly used by successful people to turn thoughts into reality. Although this is a mental exercise, it is a form of spiritual innovation. This is also a formula that will continually yield success in your life.

By steadily practicing positive visualization, self-analysis, and meditation, any Yoga student should be successful within any chosen path taken during the course of his or her life. You will notice that I mention "positive" visualization. Do you think that Tiger Woods ever focused on missing a putt or losing a golf tournament? Whatever you envision, can easily become your reality.

Therefore, always focus on achievement and success. You cannot afford to think of anything else. See yourself overcoming obstacles and living your dreams. This is what all achievers do.

Now, let's take a closer look at intuition. If you are not an intuitive person, you should work on enhancing this quality.

Balancing Ajna chakra might help you, and if this is not a possibility, you should keep a trusted intuitive person around you, when it is time to make important decisions.

This is not to say that intuition is the overriding factor in your decision making, but intuition always has weight. Intuition will help us seek and find the deeper truth in all matters. This allows us to develop our personal awareness of what is, what is not, and what could be.

As we continue our journey to find the deeper truth, we become much more aware of the many possibilities and opportunities we have to contribute to the common good of all.

Astrology of the Chakras

It is well known to many of us by now that the "human energy field" is comprised of seven major energy centers or chakras that are located along the cerebral-spinal axis. Each of these centers acts as a substation or transformer of the universal energy or prana that flows through the medulla at the base of the skull. As the prana descends through the five lower chakras it is transformed or modified from it's pure state. If the lower chakras are clear and free of negative impressions (trauma, suppression, etc.) then the prana is free to ascend back to the upper chakras leading to higher states of consciousness.

If the lower chakras are blocked, however, then the prana is blocked from ascending and these energetic blockages begin to manifest as "dis-ease" on mental, emotional and physical levels. In other words, if we have blockages in any of the chakras it means we have broken our "attune"-ment with universal life force energy on a subtle, or not so subtle, level. Since the chakras are energy centers that respond to vibration, one of the ways that we can come back into alignment or attunement is through the conscious use of vibration, music and movement.

One of the tools that can help us in this journey is an understanding, through the use of astrology, of the relationship between the chakras and the planets. In the astrological world each of the chakras is associated with or is governed by a different planet. On an energetic level the astrological chart is a map of not only the inter-relationship of the planets but a map of the inter-relationship and condition of the chakras. In essence, we have our own inner solar system that guides the evolution of our consciousness through the various chakra centers. By understanding the planetary quality of each chakra we can use specific forms of music, vibration and movement to awaken and open each chakra and energize ourselves.

✓ Astrology of the Chakras

The first chakra, located at the base of the spine, is associated with the planet Saturn. Astrologically, Saturn represents our ability to ground ourselves so that we can materialize our dreams. Not enough Saturn in our lives leaves us ungrounded and unable to support ourselves. For some, too little Saturn makes it hard to create a sense of strong boundaries and center. Too much Saturn, however, and we can hold onto the material plane too much and resist change because of insecurity and fear. One of the ways to heal the first chakra is through connecting with the energies of the earth . Walking barefoot, doing yoga and drumming are all ways of tuning into the lower frequencies of the first chakra. Drumming, in particular, is an effective way of opening and awakening the first chakra. When we drum we often hold the drum between our legs which directly connects with the first chakra at the base of the spine. By tuning into the lower frequencies of the drum we not only energize ourselves but also become more present and in our bodies.

The second chakra, governed by Jupiter, is located in the pelvic or genital region of the body. The second chakra has to do with issues of creativity and sexuality and how we channel our fundamental life force energy and emotions. Astrologically, Jupiter is the planet that represents how we expand our consciousness. If we grew up in a family that suppressed emotions or sexuality then this would directly impact the second chakra and our sense of expansiveness. If we suppress one area of the second chakra, say sexuality, then all of the other areas;: our passion, creativity, expression of deep emotion, are affected as well. When the second chakra is open we are in touch with our primal life force, or kundalini energy. This is the fundamental electromagnetic force that animates our bodies and when freely expressed creates magnetism, passion, and true creativity in our lives.

The key to awakening the energy of the second chakra, then, is to get our instinctual energy moving and open and expand the range of pelvic movement. One of the best ways I've found to accomplish this is through free form dancing or African dance forms. Several years ago I had a guest African dancer in my Astrology of the Chakras class and she explained that many of the movements of African dance are actually meant to facilitate the opening of the various chakras. Any movements that contract and then expand the area of the second chakra, or pelvis region, will help to loosen up the energy in that center. Also, using ethnic or world music that activates the instinctual or moving center, such as didgeridoo, belly dance or Turkish dervish music, are excellent.

The third chakra, located at the solar plexus or "hara" is the seat of our personal power. Mars, the planet associated with personal will and Pluto, the planet associated with collective will, are the co-rulers of the third chakra. The issues of the third chakra have to do with power, control, trusting our gut level instincts, and our sense of personal empowerment. A blocked third chakra may manifest as a lack of being able to make decisions, not being to trust our own instincts, and feelings of being manipulated or victimized. An overactive third chakra may manifest as control issues, intimidation, rage, or violence. The key to healing the third chakra is to learn how to take power without harming others. It is also important to learn how to let go of the fear of being out of control.

Music can be a particularly powerful medium for opening the third chakra as it is a non-verbal form of communication that by-passes the cognitive mind and directly impacts our deepest emotions. Many people who feel they have to control their emotions find themselves being moved to tears by evocative music. Finding music that moves you, whether emotionally or physically is a way of accessing the deeper emotions of anger, grief and rage that are often trapped in the third chakra. As these emotions are uncovered and allowed expression, the third chakra can then blossom and the energy that has been channeled into control can now be re-routed into more fulfilling forms of self expression and creativity.

✓ Music of the Heart

The fourth chakra, located around the heart and lungs, is governed by the planet Venus. Venus represents what we value, what we are passionate about and our capacity to share our love unconditionally. I also assign "higher" rulership of the fourth chakra to the planet Neptune, as it is Neptune that represents the process of transcending our own individuality and merging with spirit or divine love.

The fourth chakra is the bridge between the lower and higher chakras. It has been said that our western culture primarily relates to the issues of the first three chakras; money, sex and power. As we clear the emotional attachments of the first three chakras then we can begin to open to the expansive qualities of the higher chakras. If the fourth chakra is blocked we might have fears of not being loved, fears of giving and receiving affection or relationships that are unfullfilling.

The key to healing the heart chakra is through the development of compassion, devotion, and a sense of connection with others. Music, in the form of devotional singing, can open the heart and decrease feelings of separation. The Dances of Universal Peace from the Sufi tradition of Samuel Lewis are an excellent way of combining sound and movement to facilitate a sense of mystical connection or oneness with others. Combining sacred mantras from different spiritual traditions with simple circle dances, the Dances of Universal Peace help us to let go of the artificial walls that keep us separate. They are also a very safe way of practicing how to give and receive love unconditionally.

✓ Opening the Throat, Third Eye & Crown Chakras

The fifth chakra, located in the throat region, is governed by Mercury, the planet representing all forms of communication and Chiron, the planet representing the mentor/teacher archetype. It is through the fifth chakra that we develop personal expression and the ability to create our own reality. If the fifth chakra is blocked then we might have fears of asserting or speaking up for ourselves. It may also be difficult to express our needs or the feelings that we experience emanating from the heart chakra. Another common manifestation of a blocked fifth chakra is disbelief in our ability to create our lives the way we want them to be. If we grew up having no voice in the choices that were being made for us or having our choices ridiculed then eventually we stop believing in the power of our free will or voice.

Healing the fifth chakra is imperative if we want to open to the intuitive awareness that comes from the sixth and seventh chakras. If the fifth chakra is blocked we may be overly mental and not open to the subtle intuitive information that is constantly being channeled through the higher centers. In terms of healing modalities, singing is one of the best methods for opening the fifth chakra. Since many people with fifth chakra blockages have literally "lost their voice", the greatest way to reclaim our voice is to vibrate it with sound! Chanting sacred mantras such as OM is also beneficial as OM is seen as the fundamental, or primordial sound of the universe. As we chant OM we align ourselves with the creative sound that is thought to bring all material form into existence.

The sixth chakra, located in the middle of the forehead between the eyes, is co-ruled by the Sun and the Moon. The sixth chakra is associated with our higher mental abilities of introspection, self-examination, perception and intuition. Traditionally, the sixth chakra is seen as having two poles. The moon pole, located at the medulla, is where receive the "breath of god" or universal energy. The sun or active pole, located at the third eye, is where we express this universal energy through the vehicle of our own individuality. A blocked sixth chakra may manifest as fear of looking inside ourselves, fear of using our intuitive abilities, refusal to learn from life's experiences, or the inability to access inner guidance. Physical symptoms could include migraines, anxiety, depression and learning disabilities. One of the best ways to open the sixth chakra is through meditation, visualization and accessing the imaginal realm through dreamwork. This opening can be facilitated by music that evokes the imagination and opens us to the realm of non-ordinary insights. Specifically, there are many CD's available that help the brain to access deeper states of alpha, delta and theta consciousness that are otherwise only produced through meditation practices.

Lastly, we reach the seventh chakra, located at the top or crown of the head. The crown chakra is viewed as another point of entry of life force energy and represents our connection with universal consciousness. I associate the seventh chakra with the planet Uranus, as it is Uranus that represents the universal current of energy that nourishes mind, body and spirit. From the Vedic perspective of India, Uranus represents the kundalini energy that resides at the base of the spine in the first chakra. As we awaken and open each of the chakras the kundalini energies rise up the spine and activate the seventh chakra leading to enlightenment or illumination. Many of us experience this in orgasm as the kundalini moves through the lower chakras and activates the crown chakra. The reason we go to sleep after orgasm is that we are not used to channeling that much energy in the higher centers so we end up shutting down, or going unconscious.

If we have blockages in the seventh chakra this may manifest as low life force energy, disbelief that we can be supported by the universe, or feeling disconnected from a sense of meaning or direction in our lives. The interesting thing about the seventh chakra is that it is the polar opposite of the first chakra so we can open it from "above" or "below". Pranayama or breathing practices help to open the seventh by expanding our capacity to channel energy through the top of the head. As we expand our capacity to channel energy we can withstand more aliveness moving through our bodies without resistance.

As we open the lower chakras through movement and sound we decrease the resistance we have to being more alive and release the kundalini energy that is dormant at the base of the spine. In other words, opening the higher chakras does not mean that we need to ignore or "transcend" the lower chakras as some traditions would have us believe. Rather, it requires that we work on opening up the entire chakric field so that we have the capacity to experience higher states of consciousness in a grounded or embodied way.

Chakra Frequencies - Why Chakra Frequencies Are Important

The fact is, each chakra has its own unique frequencies. In fact, pretty much every material thing in this whole world does. Whether it be a rock, tree, human being, or dog. This Earth we live on has it's own natural frequency. And just like the earth's, a person in a meditative state has a natural frequency of approximately 7.8 hertz. This is called the Schumann Resonating Frequency. In the chakra system, our chakra frequencies need to be balanced and properly resonating throughout the body. This is key to our overall physical, mental,emotional, and spiritual health. If they are balanced, we feel at peace and everything is working together in harmony. If a frequency is off balance, it throws our whole chakra system off.

Unfortunately, our chakra system is so delicate and the balance can easily be thrown off. Something as trivial as a stressful occurrence at work, a sudden change in the weather, or even a minor illness is enough to scramble these frequencies. We need to perform regular maintenance on our chakra system by listening to the frequencies of each chakra so that they can naturally fine tune themselves back to their correct settings.

You may be wondering what kind of real effect listening to a frequency can have on a person?

I'll use an example we are all familiar with. Remember back in school, that god awful sound that comes from nails being scratched against a chalkboard? How did it make you feel? The hairs on the back of your neck probably stood up, and you covered your ears and cringed. What kind of effect that would have on you if you had to listen to that for a whole minute? The tone itself is powerful enough that it literally changes the rate of vibration in the cells of anybody who hears it.

Listening to chakra frequencies is a way to experience these vibrations in a positive and pure form. It is a form of therapy that has the power to bring our chakras back into perfect balance and harmony. When our chakras are in balance, our physical,emotional,and mental self is in balance as well.

Advanced Chakra Therapy and Cancer

Advanced Chakra therapy is based on the precept that all disease is caused by imbalanced energy. Everything in the Universe is made up of energy. Energy itself is a combination of vibration and information. Energy itself is neither good nor bad - only balanced or imbalanced. What may be a positive charged energy for one person may in fact in be a negative charged energy for another person. Same energy - different results.

Advanced Chakra Therapy perceives science is the one magic that works. There is always an authority that is stronger than the one in charge. There is always a place with those present at this moment. Thus, the reality in dealing with dis-ease using this additional therapy is not what you do with the medicine of traditional nature but it is what you allow the medicine of traditional nature to do for you.

There are 4 pathways used in Advanced Chakra Therapy. Briefly there is the Elemental Pathway. This is your physical existence. The second pathway is the Creative or Imagination pathway. This is your intuitive level and your own innate capacity to create and heal yourself. The third pathway is the Power pathway. This works with the innate healing powers to heal through intention and manifestation. The fourth pathway is the Divine pathway. Simply awakening to the unconditional love.

The Advanced Chakra therapy works with 11 different chakras. Each chakra serves as a portal and converts fast energy to slow energy. Integrating quantumn physics into the pathway formulations allowing each chakra to be programmed energetically. This Advanced Chakra Therapy is a powerful addition to the traditional medicine for disease's such as carcinomas, malignancy, and other forms of cancer, HIV, immunological diseases, and organ distress related disease.

The benefits of Advanced Chakra Therapy are immeasurable. Reports have shown that this ancient art of healing works on levels of the person enabling the traditional methods to do their jobs. Advanced Chakra Therapy is not a replacement treatment, but rather an additional content to the therapy and treatments used by traditional medicine. It allows your body to allow the medicine's work with you in a balanced and harmonious way.

Kundalini Dance Through the Chakras - Awaken Your Kundalini Energy

Kundalini TM Dance is a shamanic ecstatic dance journey into the seven chakras. The energetic centers in your subtle body that trigger emotions and channel life force to the vital organs, each chakra governs different organs, body parts, and specific emotions. They are gateways to the different parts of ourselves, and are deeply connected to the core of who we are and how we perceive and express ourselves in our daily lives.

The Kundalini TM Dance work balances the chakra system as a whole, and so results in physical and emotional healing. Core issues relating to survival, creativity, sexuality, personal power, love, relationships, communication, intuition, and spirituality are all expressed through the chakras. Through movement and breath, our chakras are purified by the release of stagnant and repressed emotions and thoughts, all of which are energy that has become trapped in the mind and body. Moving and breathing through these contractions creates a sense of expansion, personal freedom, and inner peace, leaving you feeling cleansed, positive, and energized.

The breath is a powerful tool for transformation; it's the key to physical, emotional and spiritual well-being. In the Kundalini Dance sessions the chakras become our journey map; we breathe into them and dance them awake. Shake it up to break it up. As Kundalini Shakti energy rises upward, she activates and purifies the chakras. Combining the special breathing techniques that purify and express the energy of each chakra with your personal dance movements, you shift stagnant energy that has been held in the cells of the body. Through the breath we can let go of stress, anger, grief, fear, and negativity. It rejuvenates the body, bringing insight and clarity to the mind, and supports the awakening of higher consciousness.

Healing Sacral Chakras on Animals

Pet's and animal's need our healing capabilities just as much as humans do. They have emotional, spiritual, physical, and mental issues and ailments too. Unfortunately we do not always understand or see them until they are so far to one extreme or the other due to a major communication gap.

But no matter when or where the animal is on its healing pathway, it can be helped with a variety of different healing techniques. You can use crystal healing, energy or vibrational healing, massage techniques, acupuncture, and many more to help our animal companions in our life.

The animal's second chakra, also know as the sacral chakra, is located in the lower back region between the tail and the middle of the back. This chakra center is associated with the color orange and works on issues with expression, emotional balance, control and sexuality. When working on animal's, and with an imbalanced chakra or a chakra blockage these signs can be shown as being overly emotional, hormonal issues, boundary issues with people as well as other animals, and can also be excessively vocal, including purring, whining, squawking, hissing, barking, howling, meowing, and many more.

For healing the second chakra area, you want to use whatever combination of healing techniques that feels right for you and the animal that is needing some help. Preferably use crystal vibrational healing for animal sessions. Working with Carnelian, Orange Calcite, and Coral are wonderful stones for this purpose. Make sure to cleanse the stones before and after each session, as you do not want to pass along energy to another animal or human from a prior session.

The Chakra System - How to Care and Maintain Them - Three Levels

Here we will be looking at the three levels of Chakra maintenance. Looking after your chakra system well can make a significant difference for anyone, however, if you work with people on a daily basis, especially if you are in a caring or healing role (for example nursing, teaching, healing, shop work), your energy gets pulled out of alignment every day as your focus is on others. To cleanse and re-align your energy with your self on a daily basis will make a huge difference to your life.

In a broad sense, there are three levels of Chakra Maintenance and Care.

The first level is Self Maintenance. At this level you are taking responsibility for your Chakra System on a regular basis, in the same way you shower, wash your hair and brush your teeth. There are many ways to do this, the most effective involving visualisation and other Mind-

Based techniques to cleanse, balance and align the chakras both individually and as a system. You do not need to have huge psychic powers to do this, and if you struggle with using your imagination, there are other options, but more about that later.

The second level is General Treatments. These are usually offered through beauty and massage salons, many Reiki practitioners and other healers and health practitioners offer a range of treatments designed to balance, align and attune your chakra system, restoring it to its healthy balanced state. This is great for most situations, a quick tune-up by a professional leaves you feeling great and keeps you balanced and grounded (if done well). Please note that when looking for a good Chakra Balancing or Chakra Clearing treatment, make sure that the therapist knows what the chakra system is. As Chakra Treatments have become increasingly popular, there are some Beauty Salons and Massage Therapists, who whilst offering the Treatments, don't even know what a Chakra is. A good indication of a therapist who is more likely to know something about the energy system is if they are a qualified Reiki practitioner (or another Energy healing practitioner) of at least level one.

The third level is Energy Surgery Treatments. Energy Surgery is specialised treatments by practitioners who are well versed in the human energy system and can delve into the chakras, removing problems, repairing damage and otherwise restoring the health of a damaged system. This work is about deep level change in your life. If you are unable to push past an issue, if you are not living the life you want or if you are under psychic attack, this work may be ideal for you. It is not usually short term work, so if you are going to do this, make sure you are committed. Many shamans and other High Level Healers are well versed in this work. It is important to pay attention when you are selecting the healer you will be working with. When reading their information or talking to them, make sure they feel genuine to you, and that you feel 'right' about this. It's not so much about promises they're making, but about whether they gel with you. For most practitioners, this work can be done long distance, over the phone or the internet without any loss of power and effectiveness. Some practitioners will even teach you some of the simpler work you can do to look after your own system, which can be a real gift!

Balance Your Chakras With Acupressure

Holistic healers have brought together the ancient wisdom of both Chinese and Indian medicine by using acupuncture in conjunction with balancing the chakras, which supports physical, emotional and spiritual health. A variation on this is to balance your chakras using acupressure and essential oils.

Acupressure, as the name suggests, substitutes applying pressure to the key points of the body instead of using needles, as in the classic practice of traditional acupuncture.

A number of studies indicate some very beneficial uses of acupressure.

One study suggested that treatment with the Tapas Acupressure Technique, for example, can help people recover and maintain their health and functioning. Acupressure may help with nausea, while another study found that it may be more effective than the most famous massage therapy of all, Swedish massage. Using fragrant essential oils brings in the power of aromatherapy in order to complement the traditional Chinese and Indian holistic remedies.

The concepts underlying the use of acupressure to rebalance the seven principal chakras are almost the same as in acupuncture. The difference is that touch takes the place of the insertion of acupuncture needles at the relevant "acupoints." These points are broadly equivalent to the seven chakras described in the Indian healing philosophy.

In aromatherapy, different fragrances are associated with different qualities and resonances, or vibrations of energy. They can be used on any part of the body or released into the air, where they counteract the pheromones that people give off, especially in stressful situations.

The idea behind using aromatherapy in tandem with acupressure is that effectiveness is mutually enhanced by matching the powers and properties of particular oils to the different potency centers that are represented by the seven chakras. These are located along the midline of the body, corresponding with points along the spine, from the head to the groin. The word chakra means 'wheel' but in Hinduism and Buddhism the chakras are also envisaged as flowers that can be opened like a blossom - in this case, through the use of fragrant oils.

Different practitioners may recommend different oils, or different blends of oils, for use on the different chakras. For example, the third chakra is associated with the digestive tract. Therefore holistic healers will select an essential oil that is believed to act upon the digestive system, such as peppermint oil. Using oils and acupressure together is a way of 'doubling up' on the effectiveness of the therapy.

Acupressure with essential oils can rebalance your chakras, releasing the flow of yin and yang by working together to integrate mind, body and soul.

Foods That Help Balance The Crown Chakra

Crown chakra also known as Sahasrara, is the seventh of seven chakras. Sahasrara is one of the most important parts of your inner being. It helps in connecting and the release of karma, physical action with reflection and intellectual action with the universal consciousness and unison. It is also known for its strong emotional action with 'being-ness' and detachment form illusion. This crown chakra is located on your head top. Usually, it is said to radiating golden, lavender and sometime white colors. This part also acts as your conduit especially when there are some forms of peace associated energies that are flowing in your inner being. It is therefore important to always protect it in term of feeding it with the special food that helps it to vibrate properly.

Since your crown chakra is invisible, you need to always understand how to feed it and this is mainly determined by how you eat. During fasting, this part of your spiritual being always resonates properly in respect to the needs clarification and also purification. This information is important because it determine how your well-being affects your crown chakra. For this reason these are the various ways on how you should eat in order to maintain this chakra: always avoid food with additives and other added artificial ingredients. These include all sweeteners that are artificial, preservatives, dyes, and all other food colorings. These components are always the source of toxicity in your body which leads to blockage of spiritual energy channels in your body. When this occurs, you may end up having some symptoms such as hyperactivity, lack of focus, and also unexplainable headaches.

Another element of your foods for Sahasrara is that you should always include some gentle and important detoxes in your daily food stuffs. These detoxes are meant to cleanse your inner body especially by removing all toxins deposited in your inner channels. These toxin may not necessary be associated to the food you consume, but also to other factors like pollutions and being inactive. For this reason, you should always embrace foods that are rich in fiber. These include things like fruits and vegetables, legumes and other berries.

Before taking your healthy meals, you should make it a habitual thing to always relax, meditate and also reflect on how connectivity and purifications you are to get. Always have a short prayer that should be for thanking all what happened to the nature until that food came in to existence. This is very vital especially in acknowledging all the interconnections behind that food you are about to take.

Apart from the normal food stuffs, your crown chakra needs other special forms of foods. One of these foods is sunlight. Sun been one of the sources of universal energies, always helps the crown chakra to radiate and vibrate properly. This is important especially when it comes to nourishment of love, grace that is divine and also hope. Apart from the sunlight, oxygen has also been a very important food for crown chakra. Oxygen is essential especially when it comes to consciousness and lives of chakra. For this reason, you will always need this oxygen in order to maintain the functionality of your crown chakra. Finally love is another component that your crown chakra deserves. This love should be based to all things around you include nature, self-love, love of others, and finally love of planet. Once you follow all these instructions for your Sahasrara foods, you will be enjoying the best and perfect purifications and interconnectivities within at all times.

Balance Your Chakras With the Power of Tuning Forks

Sound healing with tuning forks can be a simple but powerful way to balance the chakras and improve the flow of energy in the body, resulting in less stress, and more energy to make life changes.

✓ How Tuning Forks Work

Quantum physics is now confirming that our bodies are not solid matter, but an orchestra of vibrational frequencies. Each cell, organ or body system has its own optimal frequency that corresponds to a health state. Illness and disease indicate that the vibrational frequency is out of balance. The specific frequencies of various sounds can change the frequency of the chakra. At a metaphysical level, aches and pains are an indication at the cellular level that the life force energy of the physical body is blocked. The power of sound can release trapped energy and make this energy available for restoring health and making life changes. Tuning forks can search out and work on blockages in the subtle energy bodies that surround the physical body and change imbalances before they manifest at the physical level.

✓ Putting it Together

There are many types of tuning forks that use different frequencies. Some are based on the current musical scale while other are based on specific numerical sequences or energies. One example is the tuning based on the ancient Solfeggio frequencies. The Solfeggio frequencies are part of an ancient musical scale that was originally part of the Gregorian Chant. Eventually these powerful frequencies were replaced with changes in the musical scale based. These frequencies have been rediscovered and are now being used to reduce stress, increase energy flow and facilitate the body's ability to heal itself.

Each of the six frequencies correspond to one of the chakras:

- 1st Chakra uses the UT Fork at 396 Hz for Liberating Guilt and Fear

-    2nd Chakra uses the RE Fork at 417 Hz for Facilitating Change
-    3rd Chakra uses the MI Fork at 528 Hz for Transformation and Miracles
-    4th Chakra uses the FA Fork at 639 Hz for Connecting to Others
-    5th Chakra uses the SOL Fork at 741 Hz for Expressions and Solutions
-    6th Chakra uses the LA Fork at 852 Hz for Awakening Intuition
-    The 7th chakra is the connection to the Universe and is the sum of the previous six frequencies

The practitioner works by having the client first lie face down on a massage table. The client hears the tone of the first tuning fork. The fork is held over each chakra to achieve balance. After the root chakra, the client hears a combination of the UT fork and the next chakra. The interval between the two forks is important. The practitioner creates an energy bridge from the root chakra to each succeeding chakra. The two forks are used to trace the intertwining energy channels up the base of the spine to the crown. The client turns over and the process is repeated, working from the crown chakra down to the root.

In summary, the chakras play an important role in balancing the energy within the body and maintaining the proper balance necessary for optimum health. Sound is an important way to restore balance to the chakras and facilitate the movement of energy throughout the body. It can be a simple but powerful technique.

Your Correct Tai Chi Practice

Like Yoga and so many other disciplines which combine the physical with the metaphysical, Tai Chi Chuan can be approached in many different ways. The motives for taking up the art are as varied as the students who practice it.

✓ Common Physical Goals for Tai Chi Practice

Improving balance - It is easy to move through the transitions of the form quickly, but much more demanding to perform them very slowly. This is the correct way. Moving slowly and gracefully helps practitioners vastly improve their balance.

Correcting back problems - In doing your form, no matter which style you have chosen, you will find yourself constantly working the entire length of the spine. Correct practice gently opens the vertebrae, reduces back pain, and encourages a healthy, more functional back.

Easing joint pain - Just as back problems can be reduced and ultimately healed by correctly doing the form, joint problems can also be reduced or alleviated. This is especially true of neck, knee and shoulder blockages.

Normalizing blood pressure - This demanding yet meditative exercise has the effect of normalizing blood pressure and heart rate extremes, and this normalization sometimes occurs within the first few months of practice.

Strengthening the legs - Tai Chi, like all martial arts, requires the strongest possible foundation. Over time, the very repetition of the slow, smooth movements through the varying positions will increase your leg strength, along with your balance.

Better breathing habits - The correct practice of your form is intrinsically connected to your breathing. For this reason, one should study the form with a good teacher who addresses diaphragmatic breathing and teaches students when they should be breathing in and out.

✓ Common Mental Goals for Tai Chi Practice

Enhanced memory -Tai Chi Chuan is not for mental sissies. Even the short forms require much detailed memorization. Your memory improves with practice, just as your muscles do. In this case, the demands on your memory are good opportunities to keep your mind sharp.

Mastery of martial techniques - Not everyone goes into the study of this art with the idea of using it as a martial art. Nevertheless, the meaning of "Tai Chi" is usually translated as "Grand Ultimate Fist." This is illustrative of the power available to those who master its techniques.

Belonging to a global community - Of all the group exercises performed the world over, Tai Chi is the most popular, by far.

Awareness and understanding of energy - Energy, Qi, or Chi, is the force that keeps us alive. How important is it, then, to develop a sensitivity to its workings?

✓ Common Spiritual Goals for the Practice

Quiets the mind - Once the form is internalized, it becomes a superior moving meditation. Its practice gives the body and mind something to do while the spirit occupies itself with more elevated matters.

Opens the chakras and energy meridians - As the student moves through the gently twisting positions, the subtle energy centers of the body are massaged and opened, along with the vertebrae.

Offers an opportunity for awakening - Well-done Tai Chi is a consummate source of awakening and union with the ineffable One. Energy flows better, health improves, and enlightenment, whatever that means to each individual, looms ever more attainable through its correct practice.

✓ Creating Your Personalized Tai Chi Practice

Your best practice for Tai Chi depends entirely on your own particular reasons for studying it. Upon reading through the motivations outlined above, most Tai Chi practitioners will embrace a combination of goals, but there will be some that are more important to you than others.

In the future, your goals will probably change, and you will be attracted to the other layers of benefits that Tai Chi has to offer. In fact, transformation is the ultimate goal, and is available to all seekers, whether they favor its physical, mental, or spiritual facets.

NOTE: The related Tai Chi Ruler practice can be performed by just about anyone, even from a seated position. It provides the same benefits as the regular form, with a focus on learning to move and use energy.

Treating Depression With Reiki

Reiki Masters believe that thought is energy vibrating at a very high frequency while the human body is energy vibrating at a lower frequency. Vibrations produce actions and actions produce reactions at grosser and grosser levels of frequency in a ripple effect!

While positive thoughts are universally acknowledged to manifest as health, negative thoughts are held to produce disease or lack of ease. Mental disease is manifested as depression, depressive psychosis, mania or even schizophrenia.

Treating depression with Reiki is fast becoming a sought-after alternative to modern drugs. Reiki deals with depression as negative energy. Negative energy manifests at the aura level as imbalance in the Chakras or energy centres and is visible to the Reiki practitioner as grey or black spots in the aura. Imbalance of the energy centres causes reactions at a physical level, for the energy centre governs the health or disease of the organs and endocrine glands located within its purview.

✓ The Chakra System and Depression

The Chakras that are usually blocked in a person who is depressed are the lower-- the root chakra, the naval chakra, and to some extent the solar plexus chakra, which is part of the middle group.

The Root Chakra anchors the person to the earth. It represents the physical will and is associated with the spinal column, bones, teeth, nails, anus, rectum, colon, prostrate gland, blood and the building of cells. The Suprarenal glands, which produce adrenalin and influence body temperature, are governed by condition of the root chakra. The person whose root chakra is out of balance cannot accept life or enjoy physical existence. The creative energy of such a person is low and self-expression is not considered necessary. The person will have a tendency to overindulge in sensual pleasures such as overeating, alcohol, sex etc. He or she becomes selfish, self-centred. Physically the person becomes overweight and suffers from constipation. When challenged the person becomes irritable, aggressive, upset, violent and displays a complete lack of trust. If the Chakra is completely blocked the person will lack physical and emotional stamina and will be filled with feelings of uncertainty.

The Naval Chakra is the creative and reproductive centre of the being. It is associated with the pelvic girdle, kidneys, bladder and all liquids such as blood, lymph, gastric juices and the regulation of the female menstrual cycle. The glands associated with this chakra are the Prostrate, gonads, ovaries and testicles. If this energy centre is active and free of blocks the person exhibits freedom in self-expression and life appears interesting. Interpersonal relationships are regarded as beautiful. A disharmonious chakra induces the person turn off sensual messages and display low self-esteem, emotional paralysis and sexual coldness. Life does not seem worth living and suicidal tendencies manifest themselves.

The Solar Plexus Chakra is the power centre of the being. A harmonious Chakra gives the person a feeling that he has the power of shaping things. It is associated with the lower back, abdomen, digestive system, stomach, liver, spleen, gallbladder and the automatic nervous system. The organ that is governed by this Chakra is the Pancreas. The body absorbs solar energy through this chakra. This nurtures the ethereal body and energizes and maintains the physical body. Emotional energy is also governed by this Chakra. Personality traits and social identities are determined by it. Since it is located between the lower and higher chakras it has the additional function of purifies the basic instincts and directing the creative energy to higher values of life. It is also connected to the astral body and helps us integrate our feelings, wishes and experiences harmoniously. A block solar plexus chakra deprives the individual of the zest for life. The person feels gloomy, unbalanced and moody. Negative vibrations impact the individual through this chakra. The person is restless and attempts to manipulate everything in accordance with his or her own wishes. There is a persistent feeling of inadequacy, which drives them to ceaseless activity. The person gets easily threatened and tends to feel dejected and discouraged. The person insists that obstacles are preventing them from realizing the true goals of life.

It is clear that the symptoms of a person in the grip of acute depression are as much physical as emotional and psychological. A block will exist in the root chakra, the naval chakra and the Solar plexus Chakra. The creative energies of the person will be at an all time low and the person will avoid situations where he or she has give expression to his or her feelings. He is self indulgent, selfish, self-centred and suffers from a large number of ailments related to the stomach and has a tendency to put on weight. He or she will lack physical stamina and will be moody, irritable, aggressive and defensive. He will have no interest in life and will refuse to socialize. In extreme cases he will attempt suicide.

✓ Combining Reiki With Other Therapies.

Many Reiki practitioners combine crystal therapy with Reiki to stimulate the chakras. Limonite, Lapis Lazuli, Pietersite, and Turquoise are used to stimulate the sacral Chakra Wardite, Mesolite, Jasper, and Jet, help the base chakra open up. The Solar Plexus Chakra is stimulated by chrysanthemum stone, gypsum, jasper, obsidian and rutilated quartz.. Wadeite is used to stimulate all the chakras. I personally, combine Reiki treatment with Bach Flower treatment and crystal therapy as I find that it accelerates the healing and gives the patient a psychological satisfaction.

As is evident from the above case study, that Reiki brings about immediate and dramatic improvement in condition of persons suffering from depression. It is also evident from countless testimonials that persons who have come out of their depression by using Reiki have not had a recurrence of the same. Many hospitals round the world are recommending Reiki as a parallel system of treatment. Treating depression with Reiki is becoming a recognized practice within hospitals and more so with local doctors. The efficacy and impact of Reiki is best understood when it is personally experienced.

Basic Chakra Exercises For Balance and Health

As much as working out is good for the overall well-being of an individual's body, so too does your chakras reap the benefits of exercises which develop and enhance them. In performing these chakra exercises, remember the primary objective should be to increase your chakra's health and balance, and in so doing increase your overall health and balance too.

Prior to conducting the actual exercises, it will be best if you silent the mind, breathing deeply and also steadily. When calm, you can now get started warming up. When you are completely warmed up, now you can carry on with the chakra exercises.

1.Root Chakra

- Lie flat on your back and bend your legs. Move your legs to the right, and also turn your head in the reverse direction. Keep the position for several counts and then try it on your other side.

- Still lying flat on your back, place your arms along your sides, bend and lift your knees closer to your head, along with your head off the floor and lifted towards the ceiling. Hold this position for three counts, then repeat two times.

- Stand up and spread your legs until you're squatting. Make certain you remain balanced, along with your feet flat on the floor. Maintain this position for several counts.

- Resume lying on the floor. Relax.

2.Sacral Chakra

- Repeat steps one and two of the root chakra exercise. Straighten your legs, hold the position for three counts, and repeat twice.

- Stand up and stretch out your arms to your side on a 30º angle. Carefully lift one foot up from the ground until it is level with your other knee. Keep on holding the position for several counts, and repeat with your other leg.

- Resume lying down on the floor. Relax.

3.Naval Chakra

1.Repeat step one of the root chakra exercise. Move onto your stomach, lift one arm and its other leg off the floor. Maintain, and repeat with your other side. Repeat twice.

2.Standing straight,breathing deeply and give full attention to your naval area. Let out your breath sharply, pushing all the air out from your lungs. Do this twice.

3. Resume lying on the floor. Relax.

Conclusion

You will be amazed at the differences you will feel once your chakras are all balanced, tuned and stimulated! Like most meditation and deep alpha, theta and delta states, it is all about getting your mind and your brain into the best range of brainwaves to perform these amazing skills and abilities.

42550125R00131

Made in the USA
Lexington, KY
17 June 2019